WORK & SOCIETY
Number 1

THE FUTURE OF THE WELFARE STATE
VOL 1

edited by
Wil Albeda

with contributions by

J.A.H. Maks
Joan Muysken
Chris de Neubourg
David Plotke
Joop Roebroek
Göran Therborn
Hans-Jürgen Wagener

Published for the
European Centre for Work and Society

by
PRESSES INTERUNIVERSITAIRES EUROPÉENNES
MAASTRICHT

The papers in this volume were originally presented as contributions to the Conference on "The Future of the Welfare State", organised by the European Centre for Work and Society and the Economics Faculty of the University of Limburg in Maastricht (NL) on December 19-21, 1984.

Production editor: Jacqueline Reason
© European Centre for Work and Society, Maastricht.
ISBN 90 - 70776 07 3 , March, 1986.

CONTENTS

INTRODUCTION

The western world as a whole has not yet left the recession behind. The welfare state as we know it in most western European nations is still wrestling with the consequences of the recession.

The depression, at least in my view, was not caused by the welfare state. However, the welfare state did not play the role that was assigned to it originally. The welfare state was motivated by agreements of solidarity and social justice. But at the same time there was an economic reasoning behind its introduction. The welfare state as an economic arrangement was seen as a guarantee for the stabilisation of its economy by the elimination of widespread loss of purchasing power in the case of the onset of a recession. The welfare state as a "built-in stabiliser". In this sense it was the outcome of the lessons of the thirties.

The development of the welfare state played a role in the unprecedented and prolonged growth of western economies since 1945. When the main political parties accepted the basic idea and were convinced of the economic feasibility, its further development was a matter of the eternal competition for votes. The welfare state is in that sense a logical outcome of development in a representative democracy. The welfare state gives the voters what they want.

The seventies and eighties saw in the first place the collapse of economic growth. There is no doubt that the welfare state did play at least part of its role as an economic stabiliser. In the thirties unemployment led immediately to poverty and widespread poverty deepened the depression. In the seventies incomes did not decrease so much and economic activity did not fall to such an alarming depth as during the thirties. However, growth rates slowed, and where (as, for example in the Netherlands) the labour force kept growing, unemployment increased sharply. The cost of the welfare state therefore increased and at the same time the revenue of the social fund and the treasury decreased. In one country after another the welfare state met with severe economic difficulty. The economic recession led to a financial crisis of the welfare state.

The financial crisis not only put an end to attempts to resolve the problem of the recession by an increase in government spending, it also led to a new discussion on the economic, social and cultural aspects of the welfare state. Of course the main argument was economic. As Plotke says in his paper, conservatives have argued that social policy blocks and distorts economic growth. This criticism has met with a surprisingly broad following especially in the United States, but in various parts of Europe too. Naturally nothing is more convincing than success, and lack of success is defeating, but still the change in thinking is striking.

The welfare state, one might say, is a form of co-existence of a market economy and a socially active state. It is this arrangement that made the political consensus on the desirability of the welfare state possible. The failure of the welfare state to overcome the depression leads to doubts about the feasibility of this co-existence. The market economy presupposes an active, individualistic and materialist society. The welfare state in the eyes of its critics leads to a society that is very different. The bureaucratic management of the welfare state discourages individual initiatives - the high levels of social security demotivate workers and the past of full employment has led to an adverse relationship between wages and profits.

Basically the welfare state undermines those human tendencies that are vital for the working of a market economy. In their paper Muysken and Wagener agree that there is no statistical evidence of a negative influence of the welfare state on either output or production and economic growth. Maks develops a theoretical framework to study the compatibility of the welfare state and the market economy. He then formulates the question "what then would be the influence in such an economy of high and progressive income tax, high profit tax, high social security premiums partly based on income prices, of an extensive social security system, to a substantial degree transferring amounts of income without relation to the premium paid, of income prices and of a massive subsidy system?" Almost a rhetorical question, one would conclude.

De Neubourg's analysis however tends to qualify this picture a little. "Recent debates tend to over-emphasise the negative aspects of social security." Empirical research in his view did not find the negative influence of unemployment benefits that could have been expected.

While rejecting the conservative critique, Plotke advocates the development of a new role of the welfare state and social policy. New technological developments demand an expansion of scientific and human service activities. Therefore social policies are necessary to develop learning capacities and to assist individuals in transition between the formal labour market and other activities. The solution, then, would be not to abolish or dismantle the welfare state but rather to change its content in such a way that the symbiosis of the welfare state and a market economy is possible again.

The typology of welfare states by Therborn and Roebroek helps us to develop a more nuanced view of the relationship between the welfare state and the market economy. I have the impression that "hard" welfare states fare better than "soft" ones. However, the different demographic trends blur the picture to such an extent that unqualified statements ready for political use are hard to make.

It is the burden of unemployment and other forms of non-economic activity that made the welfare state so much a burden for economic recovery. It might also be the specific character of the welfare state that is to blame. In the summing up of the types of welfare states by Therborn and Roebroek, two elements seem to be most important: the importance of the social security commitment; and the effectiveness of the labour market policy in preventing mass unemployment.

When the State and the social partners fail to keep some measure of full employment a financial crisis intervenes and the whole socio-political consensus as the basis for the welfare state is in danger and furthermore, the resulting dualistic economy provides the conditions for the decline of the welfare state. I tend to accept these positions. No single element in the debate is more important than the re-establishment of full employment. But is not the welfare state the main obstacle to full employment? Here political ideologies provide different answers. Personally I have the conviction that the obstacle is not so much the quantitative aspect of the welfare state (volume of benefits, financial burden) as the quality of the welfare state, its influence on the functioning of the labour market, the wage level, etc.

The welfare state is a form of economy with a human face. It is based upon the symbioses of a market economy and a socially active state. The two can survive only if they are compatible. That perhaps is the basic problem of the welfare state. Macro-economic data shows that nations with very different shares of government expenditure, such as Switzerland, Sweden and Norway and to a certain extent the United States, are able to keep a reasonable level of full employment. Why? Is it due to the demographic thrust, is it the sectorial distribution of economic activities, the lack of wisdom in wage negotiations, that makes welfare states fail?

The conference from which these papers were taken has left me with a lot of questions but I suspect that there are no simple answers. Western Europe is not yet one economy. This might be one reason for our relative stagnation. At the same time Europe is a laboratory where different forms of symbiosis between welfare states and the market economy were tried out.

Politicians, the leaders of pressure groups, and even universities should use this laboratory more efficiently, not forgetting the fascinating world at the other side of the ocean.

The conference showed some of the ways in which this laboratory can be used. But finally lessons to be drawn from the experience of ourselves and of others have sense only if we as citizens have the courage to use them, which means to choose and to act.

Wil Albeda

SOCIAL SECURITY, UNEMPLOYMENT AND THE UTILISATION OF LABOUR RESOURCES: A COMPLEX INTER-RELATION INTERNATIONALLY COMPARED

Chris de Neubourg

High unemployment rates in the seventies and eighties are partly blamed on the existence of unemployment insurance systems and particularly on the generosity of the related benefits. As unemployment insurance became increasingly discredited, the entire social security system and the welfare state were distrusted for they are said to aggravate the current problems, especially those related to employment and unemployment (1). The current theoretical and empirical discussions emphasise the impact of unemployment insurance benefits on measured unemployment. This paper broadens the scope of the debate by discussing:

a. the effects of unemployment insurance both in a partial labour market and a macro-economic context;
b. the effect of other social security acts along with the unemployment insurance system; and
c. the impact of both upon the utilisation of labour resources (2) and upon the conventional unemployment rate.

The paper emphasises the countervailing forces that are brought about by the installation and development of unemployment insurance in particular and security acts in general.

It is argued that the net impact of unemployment insurance benefits on aggregate unemployment is not only determined by their subsidisation of search and layoffs but depends equally on offsetting forces related to productive search, social customs, external economies and changes in aggregate demand and wages. As for the joint impact of several social security acts it is shown that on the one hand social security schemes may encourage people to withdraw from the labour force or reduce their effective working time (thus diminishing the utilisation of labour resources without affecting the unemployment count ne-

---

(1) This tendency is strengthened by the introduction of the 'New Classical Economic Theory' and the apparent problems of public debts in several countries.

(2) Labour resources are defined throughout the paper as the sum of all persons who are not too young or too old to supply labour services to the economy or who are not engaged in other major activities. Labour resources can statistically be defined as the population over 16 minus those following full-time education and those over 65 who are retired (see de Neubourg 1983 for details).

gatively) and that on the other hand they may increase both the frequence and duration of unemployment and urge persons to look for work who otherwise would not have done so.

The main conclusions are fourfold:
- social security systems do have an unmistakable impact upon the utilisation of labour resources and aggregate unemployment;
  there are significant international disparities in the importance and impact of various social security acts; these disparities reflect differences in legal and institutional arrangements, in standard business practice and in government policy mixes to cushion overt unemployment;
- unemployment insurance exerts a small, though significant, upward pressure on the unemployment rate; the other social security acts, however, diminish measured unemployment significantly by stimulating persons to withdraw from the labour force (by -early- retirement or -prolonged- retention in invalidity security schemes) or to reduce the number of hours effectively worked (by legitimate absence due to various reasons - including involuntary part-time work); hence, social security affects the utilisation of labour resources negatively;
- the countervailing forces brought about by social security acts are manifold and our theoretical and empirical knowledge is too casual to allow firm conclusions concerning the net impact of social security on employment, and unemployment, let alone to provide clear-cut and well-grounded policy receipts in any direction whatsoever.

The first section reviews the theoretical issues and empirical findings concerning the impact of unemployment insurance on aggregate unemployment. Explanations for the relatively small net effect are sought both in a partial labour market and a macro-economic context (section two). The scope of the discussion is broadened in section three which studies the likely impact of other social security acts and their joint effect on labour utilisation. Section four finally compares the impact of major social security acts on the utilisation of labour resources internationally. A small concluding section is added.

1. Unemployment and benefits: a complex inter-relation

The increase in the aggregate level of unemployment due to the existence and the generosity of unemployment insurance benefits was a popular theme in discussions among professional economists and among amateurish party-guests and pub visitors during the last decade. The hypothesis is consistent with recent theoretical developments such as the search theory, the natural rate of unemployment and the rational expectation hypothesis and fits in the framework of what Feldstein calls "a New View of Unemployment." This "new view" states that most unemployment consists of flows of persons who are unemployed for short periods rather than stocks of persons who are unemployed for long periods. The instability of employment, the brevity of unemployment spells and the large flows into and out of unemployment have been emphasised (3). Aggressive arguments and moral sentiments (4) entered the debate and lead to extremely contradictory empirical conclusions as found in e.g. Marston (1975) on the one hand (5) and Benjamin and Kochin (1979) on the other (6).

Unemployment Insurance Benefits are assumed to provide a major work disincentive and to raise aggregate unemployment in three distinct ways: firstly, they may cause an increase in the unemployment incidence, secondly they tend to lengthen the duration of unemployment and thirdly they induce persons to stay in the labour force. Each of these effects will be discussed seperately.

The inflow into unemployment is assumed to increase due to the existence of (or the rise in) unemployment benefits either because workers quit their job voluntarily in order to engage in subsidised search to find a higher wage, or because employers are stimulated by unemployment insurance to use temporary layoffs to cushion the impact of fluctuations in the production more often. The job search theory and the theory of contracts suggest the first behaviour to be common practice among jobholders and provide explanations of why persons rationally choose to be unemployed some of the time (hence why a good deal of aggregate unemployment has to be interpreted as voluntary unemployment) (7). It is clear that unemployment insurance benefits are of crucial importance within this view since the monetary costs of quitting and searching for a higher waged job

---

(3) See Feldstein, 1973, 1975, Hall 1972, Perry 1972, Salant 1977.

(4) The most striking example is found in Grubel and Walker (1978, p. 15): "...we acknowledge the fact that people have in effect modified their life style in response to the tremendous income potential of the (unemployment insurance) system .... they engage in leisure activities, ranging from sleeping in late in the mornings to extreme abuses, such as taking holidays skiing or in tropical climates .... In the case of working women they may be doing regular housework."

(5) Marston (1975, p. 40) "... not a figure that supports the notion of armies of unemployed malingers and chiselers."

(6) Benjamin and Kochin (1979, p. 468) qualify the army of unemployed in interwar Britain as "willing volunteers."

(7) Early contributions are found in E. Phelps et al. 1970 and G. Stigler (1961); more recent studies in the search theory include R. Gordon (1973), Hall (1972), Mortensen (1970), Perry (1972) and Phelps (1972); Bailey (1974) and Azariadis (1975) are pioneering papers explaining the implicit contract theory.

are reduced considerably. Hence they may provide a major incentive for workers to engage in this subsidised search instead
of staying at their current jobs. Empirically this effect is found
to be either extremely small or non-existent. Clark and Summer (1975), Marston (1975) and Nickell (1979) observe that relatively few persons quit their job voluntarily in order to become an unemployed searcher. These findings can easily be understood since firstly workers are under virtually no current insurance scheme entitled to receive a benefit after quitting voluntarily their job and secondly a new job can easily be found
without quitting the one held. In fact most job changes occur
without intermediate unemployment (8).

Feldstein (1973, 1975) and Bailey (1975) argue that unemployment insurance provides an incentive to the employers to
organise the production in a way that increases unemployment
by aggravating seasonal and cyclical variations and by making
casual and temporary jobs too common. Workers are not reluctant to accept being laid off because they know they will be re-
employed by the same firm after a certain period (85% of the
workers that are laid off are recalled by the same employer -
Feldstein, 1975). In the meantime they receive a benefit of
about 2/3 of their previous income, they do not search for another job and rarely accept other permanent work. In fact "temporary layoffs" should be interpreted as quasi-permanent employment (9). Empirically Feldstein found that temporary
layoffs form a substantive and increasing part of total unemployment (1975, 1978). His conclusions are confirmed by the
study of Medoff (1979) who investigated the differences between the unionised and non-unionised sector (in the unionised
sector workers are assumed to be more confident of being recalled after being laid off). Their findings, however, are strongly and convincingly attacked by Clark and Summer (1975),
Akerlof and Main (1981) and Akerlof (1979). Clark and Summer found, after a thorough study of the relevant statistics for
1976, that the temporary layoff model can account for no more
than a small fraction of the observed unemployment (p. 51) (13
per cent of total unemployment in 1976; half of these workers
return to their original employer). Akerlof and Main (1981)

---

(8) Moreover, employers tend to discriminate against unemployed workers
in favour of those having a job already. It can also be argued that voluntary re-
signation is counter-cyclically biased, since under the assumption of risk aver-
sion workers tend to stay at the job they hold during a recession.

(9) The main reason why the employers try to lay off rather than fire temporary redundant workers is the preservation of firm specific human capital. This
includes specific technological know how, the management knowledge of the
worker's ability and reliability and friendships within the workforce (Feldstein,
1975).

and Akerlof (1979) show that the figures produced by Feldstein and Medoff are more the outcome of statistical artefact than a reliable estimate of the correct magnitude of the phenomenon. After re-estimation, their results come into line with those of Clark and Summer (10, 11).

The second mechanism by which unemployment insurance may exert an upward pressure upon the unemployment rate is connected with the duration of unemployment. The length of time a person tends to stay unemployed is inversely correlated with the economic hardship experienced by the unemployed. It is clear that unemployment insurance benefits reduce the money costs of being out of work. Consequently, prolongation of the individual duration of unemployment is consistent with rational economic behaviour under the existence of an unemployment insurance scheme.

Again the job search is a useful framework to explain the resulting behaviour. The theory of "moral hazard" is also very often used to explain the behaviour (Grubel and Walker 1978, Grubel and Maki 1976). Empirically the hypothesis can be studied either on a macro or a micro level. The majority of the macro studies found a substantial and significant effect of (the rise in) the unemployment benefits upon measured unemployment (12). The most pronounced results are found for Canada, the U.K. and the U.S.A. by respectively Grubel, Maki and Sax (1975), Maki and Spindler (1975), Grubel and Maki (1976), Holen and Horowitz (1974) and Komisar (1968). Empirical evidence suggests that the effect is much smaller (thought significant) in other countries (Claasen and Lane 1979, Koning and Franz 1978) (13). These macro studies, however, are seriously criticised on methodological and statistical grounds, Extrapolation beyond the range of observations (Hamermesh 1978), serious specification errors (Hart 1982) and careless interpretation of the available data (Cubin and Foley 1977) are the most convincing arguments.

Micro studies seem to be more appropriate to study the described mechanism. Almost all investigations based on micro

---

(10) The impact of the degree of experience rating in the taxing practices is an important issue in this context; it will be discussed later.
(11) Temporary lay-offs seem to be a typical U.S. phenomenon which is not popular in Europe. Besides legal and institutional constraints, there are two plausible explanations for this difference. First, in most European countries there is a "temporary short-time work" arrangement, allowing employers to deal with output fluctuations. Second, the degree of experience rating is higher in Europe than in the U.S.A. (see Hart, 1982).
(12) See Walch (1981) for a survey.
(13) The estimation of the U.V. curve for the U.K. has been controversial (see Gujarati 1972).

cross-sectional data find that unemployment insurance does cause a significant but small increase in the mean duration of unemployment (see Chapin 1971, Ehrenberg and Oaxaca 1976, Marston 1975, Nickell 1979, MacKay and Reid, 1972, Lancaster 1978, Hamernick 1978). The non-econometric results of Clark and Summer (1973) are consistent with this result.

Besides the effects an unemployment insurance may have on the number of spells of unemployment and its mean duration, it may induce persons to stay within the labour force who otherwise would not have done so. Eligibility for unemployment benefits may stimulate persons to postpone withdrawal from the labour force until exhaustion of the benefits. Marston's post-exhaustion study indicates that unemployment insurance benefits do matter in this respect, especially if the situation under the current social security system is compared with that under no system at all. Since, however, total abolition of the system is hardly a realistic policy alternative, very little conclusions about the influence of the magnitude of benefits upon aggregate unemployment can be drawn on this basis. Marston's warning that the observed behaviour may be rather due to reporting effects than to actual behaviour is illustrated by the findings of Clark and Summer (1979), who find a large degree of inconsistent reporting in the data. Their conclusion that the distinction between "unemployed" and "out of the labour force" is often blurred, hence difficult to interpret, is therefore more plausible than the suggestion of Grubel and Walker that the unemployment insurance system "stimulates persons characterized by a strong preference for leisure to register and to stay within the labour force" (1978, p. 17). Moreover, a good deal of the persons who leave the labour force after a long period of unemployment must be characterised as "discouraged"; reported unemployment underestimates actual unemployment by their number (de Neubourg, 1983). Consequently, an increase in aggregate unemployment because persons tend to stay longer in the registered labour force due the existence of unemployment benefits, should be interpreted as a partial correction for this underestimate.

Concluding this short review of the literature concerning the impact of the unemployment insurance system upon aggregate unemployment, it can be stated that a significant but relatively small positive effect of unemployment benefits upon aggregate unemployment can be observed (Marston 1975, Ehrenberg and Oaxaca 1976, Chopin 1971, Walch 1981, Clark and Summer 1975, Akerlof 1979). The greater part of the empirical evidence does not sustain the hypothesis that the major part of current unemployment is induced by the unemployment insurance system. The positive inter-relation between the magnitude of unemployment benefits and the number of beneficiaries does exist but is much smaller than could have been expected on micro-economic theoretical grounds (search theory). The explanation of this discrepancy emphasises the offsetting forces and comprises three types of arguments related respectively to the kind of considerations that are relevant within the process of rational behaviour of both workers and employers, to the aggregate outcome of individual decisions and to the indirect macroeconomic (welfare) impact of unemployment insurance.

2. Countervailing forces

The search theory emphasises the rationality of the choice in favour of receiving a benefit instead of gaining a wage, when the difference becomes smaller. Moreover, unemployment benefits subsidise job search and contribute to the mistaken real wage expectations, hence induce the unemployed to hold out for more. However, the theory ignores that it would be irrational for jobseekers to choose to remain out of work for an extended period firstly because they violate a powerful 'social custom' ('norm') and secondly because their skills, morale, physical and mental capabilities are liable to deteriorate until employers would be most reluctant to (re-)hire them.

Notwithstanding the existence of an elaborated system of social security providing transfer incomes of different types, the dominant norm in Western societies is that "in principle" one should work in order to gain an income. This norm (social custom) is sustained and reinforced by the fact that not only the money income but also status, prestige and power are distributed among the population according to whether or not a person works and the type of work he/she does. Disobedience of an accepted social custom, despite pecuniary advantage for the individual, leads to loss of reputation or, in the extreme, to the exclusion of the individual form the group that accepts the norm. In this case disobedience has a price which may be judged higher than the pecuniary advantage from it. Applying the theory of social custom developed by Akerlof (1980) (in order to explain wage inflexibility accompanied by considerable aggregate unemployment), leads to a plausible explanation of the fact that most individuals do not choose to become or stay unemployed, not even if the economic costs would be zero. The social costs (loss of reputation, prestige, status, power) and sanctions (exclusion from the group and being the victim of stigmatisation) are incorporated in the utility function of the individual and will shift the decision towards conformity with the social custom. This explains why the rationality of the search theory is not found in its pure form in actual behaviour. However, it is clear that the weights of the social costs are not independent from the number of individuals "who break the rules".

As the number of unemployed, voluntarily or involuntarily, increases, the dominant work norm will be eroded; finally "a culture of unemployment" may emerge (14).

Besides the social costs of unemployment there are economic costs for which an insurance benefit cannot account. The costs are related to the behaviour of employers, who tend to stigmatise unemployed job applicants for two reasons. First they expect the skills and abilities of unemployed workers to be negatively affected by being unemployed; secondly, they distrust unemployed workers for disobeying the dominant social custom, hence they see them as less reliable. Consequently, employers anticipate higher future costs in terms of productivity losses due to prolonged training, high turnover or insufficient morale (15) and will use "unemployment" as a screening device (16). This behaviour is acknowledged by the workers who will take the likelihood of accumulated future income losses after a prolonged period of unemployment into account in weighing acceptance of a job offer or staying at the job they hold against unemployment (17).

The complex rationality, resulting from the mechanisms described above, as opposed to the simple rationality assumed by the search theory, leads to a more complex inter-relation between unemployment benefits and aggregate unemployment. It also partly explains why the impact of the former upon the latter is found to be significant but small in empirical studies. The complex rationality model is consistent with three kinds of empirical findings. Zabalza, Pissarides and Barton (1980) investigated the determinants of retirement decisions in Great Britain and found that men are not seriously responsive to eco-

---

(14) The fact of an individual being expected to work in order to gain an income being a dominant norm in western societies does not exclude the possibility that this social custom is no longer accepted by certain sub-groups within the population. Subgroups may be prone to more disobedience, either by taste or forced by the situation (e.g. mass unemployment); this breaking of the social custom will, at least to some extent, undermine the beliefs responsible for its observance and may lead within the sub-groups to the establishment of an alternative norm. As the mechanism proceeds a "sub-culture of unemployment" may result.

(15) Which cannot be compensated for by lower wages due to the mechanisms described by Akerlof (1980).

(16) See also Beveridge (1930, p. 139): "We have always found, as to the artisan, that if he happens to be out of work for three months he is never the same man again. He becomes demoralised".

(17) Again stigmatisation by employers diminishes as more persons become unemployed, see also Spence, 1973.

nomic incentives before pensionable age (supply elasticies being low before pensionable age). This illustrates the strength of the social custom for well-defined age groups referred to above (18).

De Neubourg (1985a) estimates a UV curve for the Netherlands (1955-1980), incorporating the various assumed causes for an upward shift after 1967. From his results it becomes clear that the replacement ratio (the mean benefit/mean wage ratio) does not contribute significantly to the observed increases in unemployment due to labour market imperfections. When, however, benefits and wages are weighted with the number of beneficiaries and the number of wage-earners respectively, the ratio is a significant variable in the UV curve. This illustrates that economic incentives to become or stay unemployed are insufficient to explain rational behaviour (19). Clark and Summer (1979), finally, found that the great majority of the unemployed in the U.S.A. accept the first job offer they receive (only 10 per cent refused a job offer).

Besides the complex rationality governing the search behaviour of workers and employers, there is the standard cost-benefit approach in the decision of employers, as the more frequent use of temporary layoffs under the existence of relatively generous insurance benefits. The Feldstein-Bailey theory emphasises the advantages for firms. However, since laying off workers and paying the unemployment benefits is costly, the popularity of the instrument depends strongly on how the financial burden of the operation is paid. The degree of experience rating is most important in this context, as acknowledged by Feldstein (1976), Brechling (1981) and Topel and Welch (1980). Brechling finds that the unemployment insurance taxes constitute a relatively small proportion of the payroll. Hart (1982), however, convincingly argues that the propensity of the firm to use temporary layoffs is dependent on whether the unemployment insurance taxes have to be regarded as a fixed or a variable cost. The current taxation practices in the United States and Europe are compared; Hart concludes that the use

---

(18) Their remark that it can also be due to the unwillingness of employers to offer jobs to elderly people is nothing more than the behavioural translation for the demand side of the labour market.

(19) Moreover, the result sustains the hypothesis that an individual is more likely to become or to stay unemployed when the chance that he or she knows someone in his (her) surrounding who is already unemployed relative to the chance that he or she knows someone who is employed. In other words an individual is less reluctant to break the work ethic norm when social sanctions are likely to be less severe and are likely to be shared by a larger number of his (her) peers; his (her) actual decision depends also on the definition of his (her) reference group.

of experience rating and taxation ceilings leads to the mixed nature of the actual practice. Under this regime no well-grounded conclusions can be drawn concerning the impact of unemployment benefits upon the lay-off behaviour of the firm (20).

In any case, it is plausible that the rational behaviour of employers (i.e. the consideration of benefits and costs) does not lead automatically to more layoffs (and thus more unemployment) when unemployment benefits are guaranteed.

A second type of countervailing force that may explain why unemployment benefits have but a small impact on aggregate unemployment is related to the aggregation of individual decisions. Since not all unemployed workers are entitled to receive a benefit, there are in fact two groups of jobseekers: those who receive an unemployment insurance benefit and those who do not (generally new entrants, re-entrants and voluntary job-quitters). Neither the existence nor the magnitude of unemployment benefits has a direct impact on the behaviour of the latter group. If the members of the former group postpone acceptance of a job due to the fact that they receive a benefit, the members of the non-recipient group will fill the vacancies not accepted by the beneficiaries. It is clear that this 'displacement' effect reduces the net impact of the unemployment insurance upon aggregate unemployment (21) (Mortensen 1977, Nickell 1979).

Besides the displacement effect there may be external economies to the existence of unemployment benefits that reduce its upward pressure on aggregate unemployment. Primarily, prolonged job search may (and according to the search theory, will) lead to a better match on the labour market. This in turn causes a rise in productivity and a decline in future unemployment; in other words prolonged search is productive and reduces unemployment in the longer run (Walch 1979, Ehrenberg and Oaxaca 1976). Secondly, the unemployed act as a "spare tyre" for employers. "Thus, unemployment insurance may be just what is needed to compensate unemployed workers for providing that service" (Hall, 1975, pp. 50-51). Thirdly, higher

---

(20) Hart (1982) admits that the influence of unemployment insu rance benefits on layoffs may be larger in the U.S.A. than in Europe due to considerable differences in the level of the ceiling.

(21) Mortensen (1977) argues that there is an incentive for the individuals who are not qualified to receive a benefit to reduce their reservation wage by more than if they are qualified for benefit. This enables them to find a job more quickly. The net impact of the insurance system upon aggregate unemployment depends therefore on the relative quantitative importance of the 'eligible' and the 'ineligible' groups and on the elasticity of the reservation wage to the unemployment benefit.

unemployment may serve as a discipline device for the other workers, thus reduces shirking and raises productivity (Shapiro and Stiglitz, 1984, Calvo 1981, Solow 1982) (22). Forthly, unemployment benefits have a work incentive effect by keeping some unemployed in the labour force and therefore reduce the loss of human capital.

A final type of countervailing force which probably reduces the impact of benefits upon aggregate unemployment, is related to the macro-economic (welfare) implications of the insurance system. It is clear that unemployment insurance affects aggregate demand, savings, wages and income distribution. The net impact of benefits upon employment and unemployment in this context cannot be understood without mathematical and econometric modelling. While its impact on aggregate demand and income distribution may maintain and stimulate employment, its effect on savings and wages are more difficult to understand intuitively and are themselves subject to offsetting forces (23).

Summarising what has been said so far, it is clear that the unemployment insurance system is bound to have an impact on employment and unemployment, not only because the unemployed no longer experience the pressing needs of subsistence. Empirical evidence, however, suggests that the impact upon aggregate unemployment is quite small; it seems that rather the existence of unemployment benefits more than their level determines the relationship. In this paper the small effect of unemployment insurance upon aggregate unemployment is explained by the existence of powerful offsetting forces, found in the persistence of social customs, the anticipating behaviour of workers and employers, the aggregate outcome of individual decisions and macro-economic linkages. If other social security arrangements are introduced in the analysis, the picture becomes even more complex.

---

(22) On the other hand Shapiro and Stiglitz (1984, p. 434) argue that unemployment benefits increase the equilibrium unemployment rate . . . . "In our model, the existence of unemployment benefits reduces the "penalty" associated with being fired. Therefore, to induce workers not to shirk, firms must pay higher wages. These wages reduce the demand for labor".

(23) On the one hand wages are depressed by the "implicit contract effect" (Bailey 1974, Azariadis 1975); on the other hand wages are pushed up because the reservation wages increase due to unemployment benefits. This effect is, however, smaller as aggregate unemployment increases (and reservation wages are adjusted downwards) and as the ratio beneficiaries/non-recipients declines, since the non-recipients lower the reservation wages. As to the effects on saving Korkela and Virén (1983) found no influence of social security on household savings; their results are in line with Barro and MacDonald (1979) and with Kopits and Gotur (1980), but are in contradiction with Feldstein's findings (1977, 1980).

3. .... an even more complex inter-relation

There are many social security arrangements that have impact upon employment and unemployment. Since some of
them tend to increase unemployment and others tend to lower
unemployment, it is relevant to enlarge the study and to consider the effects of several security acts. The need for this extension is more pressing in an international comparative context
since some social security arrangements may be used as an alternative for unemployment insurance. This is especially the
case where policy-makers either promote (early) retirement
and involuntary short-time work (involuntary part-time work
for economic reasons or due to labour sharing policies) to cushion overt unemployment or allow invalidity insurance to include a pool of hidden unemployed. Under these circumstances
it is myopic to limit the analysis to the impact of unemployment
insurance alone. In this selection the likely impact of social security acts related to retirement, disablement and to absence
from the job due to illness, bad weather, personal (civic) reasons and economic reasons, is discussed.

Contrary to the debate on unemployment insurance, the
amount of literature concerning the impact of other social security arrangements is quantitatively modest. Virtually no literature exists on the (un-)employment effects of social security
acts that guarantee benefits to the workers who are absent from
their job due to personal or civic reasons, to bad weather and to
slack business (economic reasons). Generally it can be said that
the first arrangement has only a marginal influence in most
countries and that the latter two cushion the fluctuations in economic activity. Since subsidised absence due to bad weather
can be assumed to reflect small seasonal variations only, investigations focused on the influence of short-time work (Onofri
and Stagni 1979, Jusenius and Rabenau 1979, Grais 1983). According to national practices (see Grais 1983, for an overview),
short-time working may have a considerable impact on measured unemployment. This is especially the case in West
Germany and Belgium, where short-time work is a popular policy instrument. Jusenius and Rabenau (1979) calculate that the
West German unemployment rate would have been 20 per cent
higher if all short-time work would have been converted into
unemployment.

The occurrence of moral hazard is often discussed in relation
to sickness and disablement insurance (as it is in relation to unemployment insurance). Consequently, little attention is given
to the net effect upon unemployment or employment; whether
the existence and the generosity of sickness and disablement

benefits induce persons to be ill more often or to "become disa-bled" more easily, is the central question in the debate. Empiri-cal evidence on this issue is scarce, but suggests that the effect is positive, though not very big (Doherty 1979, Hambor, Lando 1974). As to the impact on employment and unemployment, it can be assumed that the existence of a disability insurance scheme has a downward influence on aggregate unemployment (24). Disabled workers who would not be entitled to receive a disablement insurance benefit, would most probably register as unemployed. Empirical studies for the U.S.A. and the Netherlands find that a positive correlation can be observed be-tween aggregate unemployment on the one hand and disability benefits and applications for disability benefits on the other (Hambor, Van den Bosch and Petersen 1982). "Disabled wor-kers (who can work) are more prone to job loss and have a more difficult time finding re-employment if they do lose their jobs. Thus, during periods of high unemployment, unemployed disa-bled people will view disability benefits as a replacement source of income" (Hambor, p. 3). This applies especially to the Netherlands where the disability insurance act states explicitly that eligibility for benefits should be judged taking the labour market prospects of the applicants into consideration and where the replacement ratio under the disability insurance act exceeds that under the unemployment insurance act. Summarising, it is plausible that a part of the beneficiaries under the disability in-surance act can be regarded as hidden unemployed, though careful interpretation of the statistics is highly necessary (25). Hence the existence of a disability insurance act lowers the ob-served number of unemployed (26).

The influence of social security upon retirement decisions is the subject of a debate similar to that on the effects of unem-

---

(24) Unemployment and sickness seem to be inversely related: i.e. the num-ber of ill workers varies counter-cyclically (de Neubourg, 1983).

(25) On the one hand the work-disincentive effect of the disability insurance scheme may be larger than the work-disincentive effect of the unemployment insurance, since the offsetting force of the dominant social custom (see section 2) is much less powerful. Disablement is considered to be a legitimate reason for being out of work; hence social stigmatisation is less severe. Moreover stig-matisation by employers is far less relevant for the individual beneficiary since disablement is more regarded as a quasi permanent withdrawal from the labour force. On the other hand, other countervailing force may work. In any case an applicant should be ill or disabled and this must be acknowledged and confir-med by a doctor. The growth of the number of disabled during the last decade may be also partly due to autonomous forces like the ageing of the population, the progress in medical diagnostics and the changing opinions about illness and disability (see Bax, 1984).

(26) Again indirect macro-economic effects may affect the net impact on employment and unemployment, since benefits and taxes affect wages, aggre-gate demand, savings and income distribution.

ployment insurance. That is to say that it is assumed and theoretically explained that the trend toward earlier retirement is at least in part the result of increased social security and pension coverage (Crawford and Lilien, 1981). Numerous empirical studies support this hypothesis (Quin 1977, Boskin 1977, Lilien 1977, Burkhauser 1977, Boskin and Hurd 1978, Burkhauser and Turner 1978). Others, however, estimated the impact on social security to be very small, while the impact of private pension plans is found to be large (see Gordon and Blinder, 1980 for the U.S.A. and Zabalza, Pissarides and Barton, 1980 for the U.K.). More recently, many governments in Europe strongly promoted early retirement by providing economic incentives (bridging the gap between the net wage and the net benefit) and institutional arrangements. Unemployment declines as a direct effect of this policy (to the extent that the vacancies of those leaving are filled again).

From the discussion in this section it becomes clear that the majority of social security acts has an influence on unemployment. This effect, however, cannot be calculated exactly since most of the insurances affect measured unemployment by reducing the labour force or by reducing the number of hours worked. In order to make this impact visible it is necessary to depart from the potentially active population (or the available labour resources) and to study the development of the population above a certain age (27). Besides the unemployment figure, other labour slack estimates describe the utilisation of labour resources in this context. Even using these instruments it is impossible to estimate the net effect of the social security arrangements, since it is impossible to account for all the countervailing forces statistically within the scope of this paper. This section is concluded with a diagram that depicts the signs of the direct effects of the social security acts upon unemployment and labour utilisation.

In Diagram 1 it can be seen that the impact of all social insurances on labour utilisation is negative, while their impact on employment is undecided where absence from work is concerned (except in the case of short-time work). Social security acts related to retirement, disability and short-time work diminish unemployment; unemployment insurance has a positive impact upon unemployment.

---

(27) More correctly, the total number of hours actually available within an economy should be the calculation basis. Since, however, not all data is yet available, the empirical information in this paper is confined to estimates in persons. For details and theoretical underpinning see de Neubourg 1983, de Neubourg 1986 (forthcoming).

Diagram 1

Insurance	Effect on	
	Unemployment	Labour utilisation
unemployment	+	−
retirement	−	−
disability	−	−
absence from work due to illness	?	−
short-time work	−	−
bad weather	?	−
personal reasons	?	−

4. .... internationally compared

It is extremely difficult to estimate the net effect of social security regulations on the utilisation of labour resources, employment and unemployment. Moreover, the relevant data is not always easily available nor organised in a useful way. This section illustrates the two main points made in section three: firstly, the impact of the existence of other social security acts exceeds the impact of the unemployment insurance; they reduce the utilisation of labour resources by stimulating people to withdraw from the labour force and by sustaining a reduction in the hours worked by the employed. These two effects tend to cushion overt unemployment. Secondly, considerable international differences exist in social security practices; these practices reflect policy decision both on the extent of the welfare state and on the instruments to reduce overt unemployment. Data on four countries is discussed descriptively that can be characterised as a primitive cliometric method (where available data for Canada, the Netherlands, Sweden and the United States are presented).

Social security arrangements related to retirement and disability tend to diminish labour force participation rates. This means that these social insurances decrease the labour force relative to the potential labour force defined as the population above a certain age. Their effect can be compared with the effect of unemployment by expressing them both as a percentage of the population older than 16 (or 15); a measure of the labour resources left unused due to unemployment and due to non-participation related to retirement and disability is obtained.

Table 1 compares the two statistics for three countries. It can be seen that the impact of retirement and disability upon the utilisation of labour resources is considerable. In Sweden and the United States their impact exceeds that of unemployment; the U.S. figures are also higher than those for Canada and Sweden.

Table 1

The number of the retired (R) plus the number of the disabled (D) and the number of the unemployed (U) as a percentage of the population older than 15 (1) (annual averages) 1960-1983

	Canada		Sweden		United States	
	U	R + D	U	R + D	U	R + D
1960	3.8		$0.1^{(2)}$	$3.6^{(2)}$	3.1	
1965	2.5		0.1	4.5	2.6	
1970	3.3		0.1	2.6	2.9	5.9
1973	3.2		0.2	4.3	2.9	6.7
1976	4.3	4.2	0.1	4.7	4.7	7.3
1979	4.7	3.9	0.1	3.5	3.7	7.9
1981	4.9	3.8			4.7	8.4
1982	7.1	3.8	0.2	3.7		
1983	7.7	3.6	0.2	3.5 .		

Sources: Canada: data provided by Statistics Canada, Ottawa.
Sweden: data provided by Statistics Sweden, Stockholm.
U.S.A.: data provided by the Bureau of Labor Statistics, Washington D.C.
(1) for Sweden: as a percentage of the population aged 16-74.
for the United States: as a percentage of the non-institutional population of 16 and older.
(2) = 1962.

Table 2 gives more detailed information on the impact of disability insurance. The figures for the Netherlands are striking in this context and reflect the effects discussed in section 3: the share of the disabled is increasing considerably due to the introduction of a new social security act. As a result the labour force is reduced by a much larger percentage than in Canada or the U.S.A.

Table 2

The number of disabled persons as a percentage of the population older than 15 (1) (annual averages) 1965-1982

	Canada	Netherlands	United States
1965			1.3
1970	1.6	2.5	1.7
1973	1.5	3.1	1.9
1976	1.9	4.0	1.8
1979	1.7	6.0	1.8
1981	1.6	6.6	1.6
1982	1.6		1.5

Sources: see Table 1. The Netherlands: see de Neubourg 1983a.

(1) United States: as a percentage of the non-institutional population of 16 and older.

Social security acts that provide benefits for the employed when they are absent from their job for various reasons became important in the post-war period. These arrangements affect the average annual number of hours worked per employee. Their overall impact on labour utilisation is reflected in Table 3 which compares the unemployment rate with the avarage number of persons absent from their job as a percentage of the labour force. From the table it can be seen that the labour resources left unused due to absence at least equal the labour resources left unused due to unemployment until 1979. After that date the impact of unemployment is larger in Canada and the United States. It is also remarkable that the impact of absence is more constant (expressed as a percentage of the labour force) in these two countries, while its impact in the Netherlands and in Sweden is growing considerably between 1960 and 1980. In Sweden the difference between the impact of unemployment is nearly 6 times smaller than the impact of absence from the job. The international differences can be explained by differences in legal and institutional arrangement and by differences in standard business and policy practices.

For illustrative purposes two more tables are added. Table 4 compares the number of absent workers due to illness between the countries: again the disparity between Canada and the U.S.A. on the one hand and the Netherlands and Sweden on the other is striking. In Table 5 the impact of absence from the job, according to the reason for the absence and the impact of unemployment is measured in hours and expressed as a percentage of the total available labour force time by the civilian labour force (for the U.S.A.) (for details see de Neubourg, 1983). Until 1981 the labour force time unused due to absence from the job in the U.S.A. was larger than the labour force time lost due to unemployment. Among the reasons for absence vacation, illness and other reasons (mainly personal and civic reasons) account for the major part. If we also add the labour force time lost by persons on part-time schedules for economic reasons, we get a picture of the likely impact of this kind of social security arrangements upon the utilisation of labour resources.

Table 3

The Number of persons with a job not at work (N) and the number of the unemployed (U) as a percentage of the labour force (annual averages) 1960-1983

	Canada		Netherlands		Sweden		United States	
	N	U	N	U	N	U	N	U
1960			12.9	.9	8.9[1]	1.7[1]	4.4	5.4
1965			13.6	.7	9.4	1.2	4.5	4.4
1970			14.6	1.1	12.3	1.5	5.4	4.8
1973			15.4	2.8	13.0	2.5	5.4	4.8
1976	6.6	7.1	17.3	5.3	14.8	1.6	5.5	7.6
1979	6.9	7.5	17.2	5.1	16.3	2.1	5.4	5.8
1981	7.0	7.5	17.9	9.1			5.2	7.5
1982	6.4	11.0		12.6	16.6	3.1	5.1	9.5
1983	6.5	11.9		16.9	15.6	3.5		

Sources: see Table 2
(1) = 1983

Table 4

The number of persons with a job not at work due to illness as a percentage of the number employed (annual averages) 1960-1983

	Canada	Netherlands	Sweden	United States
1960		5.1	3.6[1]	1.4
1965		5.7	3.7	1.4
1970		6.3	4.3	1.7
1973		7.1	4.1	1.6
1976	1.7	8.1	4.7	1.6
1979	1.7	9.1	4.6	1.4
1981	1.7	8.5		1.4
1982	1.7		3.9	1.4
1983	1.7		4.0	

Sources: see Table 2
(1) = 1963

Table 5

The number of hours left unused by persons with a job not at work according to reason, number of hours lost by the unemployed and number of hours lost by persons working part-time for economic reasons as a percentage of total available labour force time, U.S.A. 1970-1982 (annual averages)

Hours:	1970	1973	1976	1979	1982
unused by					
with a job not at work	9.3	8.7	8.7	8.9	8.2
vacation	3.3	3.5	3.7	3.8	3.6
illness	2.4	2.5	2.3	2.2	1.9
bad weather	0.4	0.7	0.3	0.5	0.6
industrial disputes	0.2	0.1	0.2	0.1	0.0
legal or religious holiday	1.6	0.4	0.6	0.8	0.5
other reasons	1.4	1.5	1.5	1.5	1.5
lost by unemployment	5.3	5.2	8.4	6.3	10.6
lost by part-time work					
for economic reasons	1.5	1.4	2.0	1.7	2.9

Sources: calculated from data provided by the Bureau of Labor Statistics, Washington D.C.

5. Conclusions

Recent debates tend to over-emphasise the negative aspects of social security; i.e. unemployment insurance benefits and other types of transfer incomes are assumed to have a substantial work disincentive effect and to raise current unemployment rates significantly. This paper does not attack the basic insights stemming from recent theoretical contributions, but argues that the inter-relation between social security and unemployment is more complex.

Empirical research found the impact of unemployment insurance benefits upon unemployment less substantial than could have been expected on theoretical grounds. This relatively small effect is explained by arguments related to the rationally social behaviour of workers and employers, to the aggregation of individual decisions and to macro-economic (welfare) countervailing effects. If the impact of other social security arrangements is crudely compared with the impact of unemployment insurance, it can be concluded that the impact of the former exceeds that of the latter. Moreover, other social security acts, in contrast with unemployment insurance, tend to cushion overt unemployment though the degree of labour utilisation is lowered by both.

Bibliography

G.A. Akerlof, 1979;
The Case Against Conservative Macroeconomics: An Inaugural Lecture, *Economica*, 1979, pp. 219-237.

G.A. Akerlof, 1980;
A Theory of Social Custom, of which Unemployment may be one Consequence, *The Quarterly Journal of Economics*, 1980, pp. 749-775.

G.A. Akerlof, G.M. Main;
An Experience - Weighted Measure of Employment and Unemployment Durations, *The American Economic Review*, 1981, Dec., pp. 1003-1011.

C. Azariadis;
Implicit Contracts and Underemployment Equilibrium, *Journal of Political Economy*, vol. 83, December 1975, pp. 1183-1202.

M.N. Bailey,
On the Theory of Layoffs and Unemployment, *Economica*, 1977, vol. 45, pp. 1043-1063.

M.N. Bailey,
Wages and Employment under Uncertain Demand, *Review of Economic Studies*, vol. 41, Jan. 1974, pp. 37-50.

R.J. Barro and G.M. MacDonald;
Social Security and Consumer Spending in International Cross-section, *Journal of Public Economics*, 1979, June, 11, pp. 275-289.

E. Bax;
Maatschappelijke verandering en arbeidsongeschiktheid, The Hague, Ministry of Social Affairs, 1984.

D.K. Benjamin, L.A. Kochin, 1979;
Searching for an explanation of unemployment in Inter-war Britain, *Journal of political Economics*, 1979, vol. 87, pp. 441-478.

F. Van den Bosch, C. Petersen;
Incidency of Disability by Sector of Industry; an Explanation, *International Social Security Review*, 1982, no. 2.

M. Boskin;
Social Security and Retirement Decisions, *Economic Inquiry*, XV, Jan. 1977, 125.

M.J. Boskin, M.D. Hurd;
The Effect of Social Security on Early Retirement, *Journal of Public Economics*, 10, 1978, pp 361-377.

I. Brechling, 1981;
Layoffs and Unemployment Insurance, in S. Rosen (ed.), *Studies in Labor Markets*, National Bureau of Economic Research, The University of Chicago Press, Chicago, 1981.

R.V. Burkhauser;
An Asset Maximization approach to early Social Security Acceptance, Discussion Paper, 463-477, Institute for Research
on Poverty, University of Wisconsin, Madison, 1977.

R.V. Burkhauser, J.A. Turner;
A Time-Series Analysis on Social Security and its Effect on
the Market Work for Men at Younger Ages, Journal of
Political Economy, 86, 1978, 701-715.

G.A. Calvo, 1981;
On the Inefficiency of Unemployment, Columbia University, October 1981.

G. Chapin, 1971;
Unemployment Insurance, Job Search and the Demand for
Leisure, Western Economic Journal, 1971, March, pp. 102-
107.

E.M. Claasen, G. Lane, 1979;
The Effects of Unemployment Benefits on the Unemployment Rate in France, in H.G. Grubel and N.A. Walker
(eds.), Unemployment Insurance: Global Evidence of its Effect on Unemployment, The Fraser Institute, Vancouver
B.C., 1978, pp. 204-233.

K.B. Clark, L.N. Summer, 1979;
Labor Market Dynamics and Unemployment: a Reconsid-
eration, Brookings Papers on Economic Activity, 1979, 1,
pp. 13-72.

V.P. Crawford, D.M. Lilien, 1981;
Social Security and the Retirement Decision, The Quarterly
Journal of Economics, August, 1981, p. 505-529.

S.S. Cubin, K. Foley, 1977;
The Extent of Benefit-Induced Unemployment in Great
Britain: some new evidence, Oxford Economic Papers,
1977, vol. 29, (March), pp. 128-140.

N.A. Doherty;
National Insurance and Absence from Work, The
Economic Journal, 1979, March, pp. 50-65.

R.G. Ehrenberg, R.L. Oaxaca;
Unemployment Insurance, Duration of Unemployment
and Subsequent Wage Gain, The American Economic Review, 1976, Dec. vol. 66, no. 5, pp. 754-766.

M.S. Feldstein;
The Economics of New Unemployment, Fall, 1973, 33, pp.
3-42.

M.S. Feldstein;
Lowering the Permanent Rate of Unemployment, A Study
prepared for the Use of the Joint Economic Committee, 93
Cong., 1973.

M.S. Feldstein;
Comments on Clark and Summer, *Brookings Papers on Economic Activity*, 1975, no. 1, pp. 49-60.
M.S. Feldstein;
The Importance of Temporary Layoffs: An Empirical Analysis, *Brookings Papers on Economic Activity*, 1975, 3, pp. 725-745.
M.S. Feldstein;
Temporary Layoffs in the Theory of Unemployment, *Journal of Political Economy*, June 1976.
M.S. Feldstein;
Social Security and Private Savings: International Evidence in an Extended Life Cycle Model, in M.S. Feldstein and R. Imman (eds.), *The Economics of Public Services*, London, McMillan, 1977, pp. 174-205.
M.S. Feldstein;
The Effect of Unemployment Insurance on Temporary Layoff Unemployment, *The American Economic Review*, 1978, vol. 68, no. 5, pp. 834-846.
M.S. Feldstein;
The Private and Social Costs of Unemployment, *American Economic Review*, 1978, 68, pp. 155-158.
M.S. Feldstein;
International Differences in Social Security and Saving, *Journal of Public Economics*, 1980, no. 14, pp. 225-244.
G.S. Fields;
Direct Labor Market Effects of Unemployment Insurance, *Industrial Relations*, 1977, vol. 16, no. 1, pp. 1-14.
R.H. Gordon;
The Welfare Cost of Higher Unemployment, *Brooking Papers on Economic Activity*, 1: 1973, pp. 133-195.
R.H. Gordon, A.S. Blinder;
Market Wages, Reservation Wages and Retirement Decisions, *Journal of Public Economics*, 1980, no. 14, pp. 277-308.
B. Grais;
Layoffs and Short-time Working in Selected OECD-Countries, OECD, Paris, 1983.
H.G. Grubel, D.R. Maki;
The Effects of Unemployment Benefits on U.S. Unemployment Rates, *Weltwirtschaftliches Archiv*, 1976, 112, no. 2, pp. 274-299.
H.G. Grubel, D.R. Maki, Sax;
Real and Insured-Induced Unemployment in Canada, *Canadian Journal of Economics*, vol. VIII, no. 2, May 1975, pp. 174-191.

H.G. Grubel, M.A. Walker;
Moral Hazard, Unemployment Insurance, and the Rate of Unemployment, in H.G. Grubel and M.A. Walker (eds.), *Unemployment Insurance: Global Evidence of its Effects on Employment*, The Fraser Institute, Vancouver B.C., 1978, pp. 1-38.

D. Gujarati;
The Behaviour of Unemployment and Unfilled Vacancies, *Economic Journal*, March, 1972, pp. 195-204.

R.E. Hall;
Turnover in the Labor Force, *Brookings Papers on Economic Activity*, 1972, 3, pp. 369-402.

R.E. Hall;
Comments on Clark and Summer, *Brookings Papers on Economic Activity*, 1975, no. 1, pp. 49-60.

J.C. Hambor;
Unemployment and Disability. An econometric Analysis with Time Series Data. U.S. Dept. of Health, Education and Welfare, Social Security Admin. Office of Research and Statistics, Staff. Paper 20.

D.S. Hamermesh;
Unemployment Insurance and Unemployment in the United States, in H.G. Grubel and M.A Walker (eds.), *Unemployment Insurance: Global Evidence of its Effect on Unemployment*, The Fraser Institute, Vancouver B.C., 1978, pp. 39-57.

R.A. Hart;
Unemployment Insurance and the Firm's Employment Strategy: a European and United States Comparison, *Kyklos*, 1982, pp. 648-672.

A. Holen, S. Horowitz;
The Effect of Unemployment Insurance and Eligibility Enforcement on Unemployment, *Journal of Law and Economics*, 17, Oct. 1974, pp. 403-432.

C.L. Jusenius, B. Von Rabenau;
Unemployment Statistics in the United States and the Republic of Germany: Problems of International Comparison, National Commission on Employment and Unemployment Statistics, Background Paper no. 30, Washington D.C., April 1979.

J.B. Komisar;
Social Legislation Policies and Labor Force Behaviour, *Journal of Economics*, 2 June 1968, pp. 187-199.

H. Koning, W. Franz;
Unemployment Compensation and the Rate of Unemployment in the Federal Republic of Germany, in H.G. Grubel and N.A. Walker (eds.), *Unemployment Insurance: Global Evidence of its Effects on Unemployment*, The Fraser Institute, Vancouver B.C., 1978, pp. 236-265.

G. Kopits, P. Gotur;
The Influence of Social Security on Household Savings: a Cross Country Investigation, *IMF Staff Papers*, 1980, March, 27, pp. 161-190.

E. Koskela, M. Virén;
Social Security and Household Saving in an International Cross-Section, *The American Economic Review*, 1983, March, 73, no. 3, pp. 212-217.

T. Lancaster;
Econometric Methods for the Duration of Unemployment, *Econometrica*, 1978.

M.E. Lando;
The Effect of Unemployment on Application for Disability Insurance, Proceedings of the American Statistical Association, 1974, Business and Econ. Stat. Section.

D.M. Lilien;
The Labor Force Participation of Older Workers, Report submitted to ASPER, Aug., 1979.

D.I. MacKay, G.L. Reid;
Redundancy, Unemployment and Manpower Policy, *Economic Journal*, vol. 82, 1972. Dec., pp. 1256-1272.

D. Maki and Z.A. Spindler;
The Effect of Unemployment Compensation on the Rate of Unemployment in Great Britain, *Oxford Economic Papers*, 1975, vol. 27, pp. 440-454.

S.T. Marston;
The Impact of Unemployment Insurance on Job Search, *Brookings Papers on Economic Activity*, 1975, pp. 13-60.

J.L. Medoff;
Layoffs and Alternatives under Trade Unions in United States Manufacturing, *American Economic Review*, 1979, vol., 69, pp. 380-395.

D.T. Mortensen;
Unemployment Insurance and Job Search Decisions, *Industrial and Labor Relations Review*, 1977, vol. 30, pp. 505-517.

J.D. Maki, Z.A. Spindler;
The Effect of Unemployment Compensations of the Rate of Unemployment in Great Britain, *Oxford Economic Papers*, 1975, vol. 27 (Nov), pp. 440-454.

D.T. Mortensen;
Job Search, the Duration of Unemployment and the Phillips Curve, *Brookings Papers on Economic Activity*, Washington D.C., 1975, 1, pp. 13-60.

C. de Neubourg;
Labour Market Accounting and Labour Utilization, Government Publishing Office, The Hague, 1983.

C. de Neubourg;
The Origin and Insignificance of Unemployment due to Labour Market Imperfections, *De Economist*, 1985, 1, pp. 64-77.

C. de Neubourg;
Unemployment, Labour Utilisation and Labour Market Accounting: Theory, Evidence and Policy, 1986, forthcoming.

S.J. Nickell;
The Effect of Unemployment and Related Benefits of the Duration of Unemployment, *The Economic Journal*, 1979, March, pp. 34-49.

P. Onofri, A. Stagni;
An Econometric Analysis of the Effects of Compensation Subsidies for Short-Time Working in Italy, in H.G. Grubel and M.A. Walker (eds.), *Unemployment Insurance: Global Evidence of its Effects on Unemployment*, The Fraser Institute, Vancouver B.C., 1978, pp. 267-289.

G.L. Perry;
Unemployment Flows in the U.S. Labor Market, *Brookings Papers on Economic Activities*, 1972, 2, pp. 245-278.

E. Phelps et.al.;
Microeconomic Foundations of Employment and Inflation Theory, Norton, 1970.

E. Phelps;
Inflation Policy and Unemployment Theory: The Cost-Benefit Approach to Monetary Planning, London, Norton, 1972.

J.F. Quinn;
Microeconomic Determinants of Early Retirement: A Cross-Sectional View of White Married Men, *Journal of Human Resources*, XII, Summer, 1977, pp. 329-346.

S.W. Salant;
Search Theory and Duration Data: A Theory of Sorts, *Quarterly Journal of Economics*, vol. 91, Feb. 1977, pp. 44-45.

C. Shapiro, J.E. Stiglitz;
Equilibrium Unemployment as a Worker Discipline Device, *The American Economic Review*, 1984, 74, no. 3, pp. 433-444.

M. Spence;
Job Market Signaling, *Quarterly Journal of Economics,* LXXXVII, 1083, August, pp. 355-374.
G. Stigler;
The Economics of Information, *Journal of Political Economy,* vol. 69, June 1961, pp. 213-225.
R. Topel, F. Welch;
Unemployment Insurance: Survey and Extensions, *Economica,* 1980, pp. 310-322.
B.M. Walch;
Unemployment Insurance and Labor Market; A Review of Research relation to Policy, OECD, MAS/WP5, 81 (1), 1981.
B.M. Walch;
Unemployment Compensation and the Rate of Unemployment: the Irish Experiment in H.G. Grubel and N.A. Walker (eds.), *Unemployment Insurance: Global Evidence of its Effects on Unemployment,* The Fraser Insititute, Vancouver B.C., 1978, pp. 172-200.
A. Zabalza, C. Pissarides, M. Barton;
Social Security and the Choice between Full-Time Work, Part-Time Work and Retirement, *Journal of Public Economics,* 1980, 14, pp. 245-276.

THE WELFARE STATE:
FROM STABILISER TO DESTABILISER?*

Joan Muysken
Hans-Jürgen Wagener

I. Introduction

In an earlier paper (Wagener and Muysken, 1984) we analysed the decline in growth performance of industrialised countries in the seventies on both sides of the iron curtain. The starting point for our analysis was Verdoorn's Law, according to which there is a positive relationship between productivity growth and production growth in industry. Such a relationship also implies a positive relationship between productivity growth and employment growth, provided that economies of scale occur. Our intuition was that when an economy is confronted with labour shortage, this second relationship would be relevant in explaining productivity growth, whereas in the case of deficient demand the first relationship would prevail. Moreover, in our opinion in the post-1970 period the economies of the Eastern bloc were characterised by labour shortage, whereas the Western economies - to some extent already in the sixties - were characterised by effective demand constraints. Using data on the Soviet Union, Poland and Hungary on the one hand and the USA, West Germany and the Netherlands on the other, we found evidence to support these hypotheses. As a consequence we explain the slowdown of productivity and employment growth in Western economies in the seventies by demand deficiencies.

Such an explanation needs two qualifications. First the question remains why effective demand does not increase to its full employment level. Second the analysis is restricted to manufacturing data whereas conclusions are drawn with respect to the whole economy. The question then is whether the impact of the remaining sectors of the economy, i.e. non-manufacturing and government, on value added and employment can be ignored in such an analysis. Little research has been done on the impact of government on the performance of the economy in a broader sense.

---

* We would like to thank H. Meijers for his computation assistance

Broadly speaking, one can distinguish between two approaches to the impact of non-manufacturing and government on the performance of an economy: the Keynesian approach on the one hand which stresses the influence of government expenditure on effective demand, and the supply-side oriented approach on the other. The tendency of studies in the last approach, which are mostly of a qualitative nature, is to explain the deteriorating performance of most Western economies from market failures and demotivating effects throughout the whole economy, caused by the expansion of the government sector and government intervention (1). Actually, both approaches emphasise two different sides of the same coin. That is, government-induced demand increases may cause market failures that cancel out, if not worse, all positive demand effects: where the non-market sector grows out of proportion it crowds out the only progressive and innovative market sector. In this context one may wonder whether the insufficiency of effective demand cannot be ascribed to an overexpanded government sector. Has the welfare state changed from stabiliser to destabiliser?

In this paper we shall try to answer these questions, focusing our attention on Western economies. We apply the analysis to six countries of different sizes and different government systems: France, West Germany, the Netherlands, Sweden, the UK and the USA for the period 1962 - 1981. The data is presented in Section 2. In Section 3 the contributions of non-manufacturing and government to value added and employment are analysed. The government sector should be defined in a broad sense with respect to its contribution to value added and with respect to market failures. That is, it should include non-market services. The impact of government in this sense on both productivity and employment is analysed in Section 4. This automatically leads to a discussion of the causes of deficient demand in Section 5.

2. Data

In the introduction three sectors of the economy have been distinguished: manufacturing, non-manufacturing and government, including non-market services. For each of these sectors we collected data on real value added and employment during the period 1962 - 1981 for France, West Germany, the Netherlands, Sweden, the UK and the USA. For each country we also have data on the unemployment rate and on the share

---

1. See for example Curzon-Price (1983) and Lindbeck (1983).

of government expenditure (including income transfers) in national income (2).

The data on real value added is published by the OECD in the National Accounts (3). The published data is subdivided into the main categories: "Industries", "Producers of Government Services" and "Other Producers". Apart from statistical discrepancies, these categories add up to GDP in purchasers' values. The largest activity distinguished within "Industry" is "Manufacturing". We identified this with the manufacturing sector in our analysis. Another activity distinguished within "Industry" is "Community, social and personal services" which we identified with non-market services. These were added to "Producers of Government Services" to obtain the government sector in our analysis. The remaining activities within "Industries" together with "Other Producers" finally constitute the nonmanufacturing sector. It is obvious that this sector is of a very heterogeneous nature. Amongst others it contains agriculture, construction and services.

The data on employment can be found in the OECD labour force statistics (4). The subdivision with respect to manufacturing, non-manufacturing and government was constructed in a similar way as in the case of value added. A summary of the data is presented in Table 1.

Before discussing Table 1 in more detail, attention should be paid to a general problem: how to define government and other non-market services in real terms? It is obvious that this problem is crucial both to the explanation of its contribution to real value added and to the analysis of the impact of government on the performance of the economy.

Since there is no market for government and non-market services, it is impossible to observe prices and quantities of these services separately. One can only observe the amounts of money used to produce these services - in particular wages and salaries - and use these amounts as a measure of the total value added of these services. This arbitrary measure has been internationally accepted for lack of a better alternative. Once using this measure, the amount of services should be related to the amount of labour employed, corrected for the productivity increase. However, due to the lack of information on quantities,

---

2. Government expenditure is defined in a broad sense: it consists of both government consumption and investment and of income transfers.
3. We used the Survey of the National Accounts for the period 1962 - 1979. The data for 1980 and 1981 was obtained from the country reports of the OECD for the various countries. For Sweden no data was available for 1962.
4. The Survey mentioned in note 3 contains an appendix with the labour force data.

such a productivity increase cannot be measured. For that reason usually a zero productivity increase is assumed, which implies that the price increase in government production is measured by its average wage increase (5). On the other hand, prices of net consumption and investment of government are measured in more conventional ways, using the price indices of the sectors with which goods are exchanged (6). Nonetheless, when looking at the data on the government sector, one should bear the arbitrariness of its measurement in mind.

In Table 1, for each of the six countries data is presented for the beginning and the end of the observation period, 1962 and 1981 respectively. The first three columns contain the shares in real GDP of the three sectors. The next three columns show the corresponding shares in employment, whereas column (7) gives total employment figures. The USA is by far the largest country. West Germany, the UK and France are approximately of an equal size, employing together about the same number of people as the USA. Finally, Sweden and the Netherlands also have almost the same size, but they are much smaller than the other countries. In columns (8) - (11) the increase in productivity is presented both for each sector and for the whole economy. The last column displays the share of government outlays in a broad sense, in national income. These shares differ widely from country to country, indicating that the selected countries do not only differ in size of total employment, but also in size of government involvement.

When we look at the shares in GDP of each of the three sectors, it is remarkable how constant these shares have remained in each country over the last two decades. Shifts of more than 3 per cent hardly occur during the period of observation. This also implies that the share of government in total real value added is more or less constant over time. Of course, errors in measurement can play a role in this context: comparison of the shares in value added and employment of government in 1962 shows that in all countries, except the USA, government productivity exceeds overall productivity in real terms in that year, which seems very implausible. However, in 1981 in all countries overall productivity in real terms is much higher. Moreover, one should not concentrate on the erors in measurement of a relatively small share of GDP: both non-manufacturing and man-

---

5. Gerritse (1979, p. 139) calculates that for the Netherlands a 1% increase in productivity implies a 0.81% increase in volume of government services.

6. According to Hilferdink (1977, p. 581), the price index of govern ment investment is taken to be that of housing construction, whereas this investment consists for its largest part of road and bridge construction which employs totally different techniques from housing construction.

Table 1: Development in Manufacturing, Non-manufacturing and Government, 1962 - 1981

	Share in real GDP (per cent)			Share in Employment (per cent)			Total employment	Increase in Productivity (1962 = 100)				Gov. outlays per cent NI
	N	M	G	N	M	G	'000 man yrs	N	M	G	T	
	(1)	(2)	(3)	(4)	(5)	(6)	(7)	(8)	(9)	(10)	(11)	(12)
USA '62	56.0	24.8	19.1	50.2	23.6	26.2	74,800					28.9
'81	58.3	24.4	17.3	52.5	18.8	28.7	109,400	1.25	1.55	1.04	1.26	35.4
BRD '62	42.7	37.9	19.5	46.0	37.5	16.5	26,534					35.6
'81	40.8	38.2	21.0	40.4	33.7	26.0	26,070	2.11	2.18	1.34	1.94	49.3
UK '62	50.3	25.7	24.0	37.6	43.2	19.2	24,632					34.2
'81	53.0	21.8	25.3	38.0	36.6	25.3	23,665	1.54	1.47	1.18	1.48	47.3
FR '62	57.0	23.7	19.3	55.9	27.3	16.8	18,820					37.0
'81	54.1	29.0	16.9	48.5	25.3	26.2	20,976	2.14	2.59	1.11	1.96	48.9
SW '62	55.5	24.3	20.2	50.8	28.5	20.7	3,665					32.4
'81	53.0	23.9	23.1	41.3	21.7	37.0	4,232	1.66	1.83	0.91	1.42	65.3
NL '62	50.6	20.3	29.1	55.5	27.9	16.6	4,243					35.6
'81	54.2	22.5	23.3	52.6	20.9	26.5	4,745	2.13	2.80	0.95	1.89	61.5

ufacturing, which are measured much more accurately, also have constant shares in the course of time in each of the six countries. As a consequence, we shall use this constancy of shares of the three sectors in GDP as a stylised fact in our further analysis. It should be noted that this constancy reflects a complementarity between the market sector and the non-market sector, which we think is highly characteristic for our welfare state. We shall elaborate on this in Section 4.

The shares in employment do not reveal such a constant pattern. As might be expected, the share of manufacturing is declining in all countries, whereas that of government is increasing. Due to the heterogeneity of non-manufacturing, its share shows different developments in different countries. The share of employment in the non-manufacturing market sector is surprisingly high in the USA, compared with the other countries. There is a remarkable difference between the variety of shares in 1962 compared with 1981. It almost seems as if the USA has set a standard in the early sixties with a share of about 26 per cent, which all countries reached by 1981. Only Sweden overshot the target. Whatever the reason may be, there are striking similarities between the shares in employment of government in 1981 between all countries.

When we look at the productivity performance, the countries show large differences. In the two decades overall productivity almost doubled in France, West Germany and the Netherlands, it increased by almost 50 per cent in the UK and Sweden and by 25 per cent in the USA. These differences are reflected in the productivity increases in both manufacturing and non-manufacturing, the latter being consistently lower. However, except for West Germany, the government hardly shows any productivity increase. This is not surprising, considering the method of real government production measurement, as we described it above. Therefore in our analysis we will also use the stylised fact that the government sector shows no productivity increase.

3. Government, value added and employment

In the previous section we inferred two stylised facts about Western economies:
– the share of manufacturing, non-manufacturing and government in real value added are constant over time. As a consequence,

$$x_m = x_n = x_g \tag{1}$$

holds, where the three variables stand for the growth rate of real value added in manufacturing, non-manufacturing and government respectively;
– government production shows no productivity increase, i.e.:

$$x_g = e_g \qquad (2)$$

holds, where e_g stands for the growth rate of employment in government.

In Wagener and Muysken (1984) we argued that the following version of Verdoorn's Law holds for manufacturing:

$$p_m = c_3 + c_4.x_m \qquad c_4 > 0 \qquad (3)$$

where p_m stands for the rate of productivity growth in manufacturing. The positive sign of c_4 is the Verdoorn effect.

An interesting explanation of the productivity growth in non-manufacturing is given in Chatterji and Wickens (1982), where they argue that:

$$p_n = c_0 - c_1.e_n + c_2.x_m \qquad c_1 > 0, c_2 > 0 \qquad (4)$$

holds. p_n and e_n stand for the growth rates of productivity and employment in non-manufacturing respectively. The negative sign c_1 is due to 'Kaldor's Proposition' that "the rate of growth of manufacturing production . . . will tend, indirectly, to raise the rate of productivity growth in other sectors" (7).

The positive sign c_2 results from the 'Externalities Hypothesis' according to which external economies of the manufacturing sector induce a positive effect of the growth in manufacturing output on the rate of productivity growth in non-manufacturing industries (8). In order to highlight the impact of output growth on productivity growth, equation (4) can be re-written as follows:

$$p_n = c_5 + c_6.x \qquad (5)$$

where $c_5 = \dfrac{c_0}{1 - c_1}$, and $c_6 = \dfrac{c_2 - c_1}{1 - c_1} . x$

stands for the overall growth rate of value added, which is equal for all sectors according to equation (1).

---

7. Chatterji and Wickens (1982, p. 21). See also Kaldor (1966).
8. Chatterji and Wickens (1982, p. 21). See also Cripps and Tarling (1973).

Equations (3) and (4) have been estimated for the six countries. In order to see whether the situation in the sixties differs from that of the seventies, we did not only estimate both equations for the period 1962 - 1981, but also for the two subperiods 1962 - 1971 and 1972 - 1981. The results are presented and discussed in Appendix 1. The most important conclusions are that Verdoorn's Law, equation (3), fits the data of the manufacturing sector well, both for 1962 - 1981 and 1972 - 1981. On the other hand equation (4) explains productivity growth in non-manufacturing poorly, except for the UK (9). However, Verdoorn's Law in the form of equation (5) with x_n instead of x, also appears to hold for non-manufacturing in both periods. The values estimated for c_4 and c_6, both for 1962 - 1981 and 1972 - 1981 are presented in Table 2, in the form of $1 - c_4$ and $1 - c_6$ respectively.

From this Table one sees that the elasticity of productivity with respect to output in manufacutring is rather high. It varies from 0.786 in the Netherlands to 0.407 in the USA, when estimated for 1962 - 1981. The corresponding figures for 1972 - 1981 lie in the same range, except for the Netherlands, where the elasticity increases to 0.982. As a consequence in the Netherlands output growth does not induce employment growth in manufacturing during the seventies. The picture for non-manufacturing is different: the elasticity of productivity with respect to output varies from 0.587 in the Netherlands to 0.899 in Sweden in 1962 - 1981. When estimated for 1972 - 1981 similar results are obtained, except for the Netherlands, where the elasticity increases to 1.044. Similar to the case of manufacturing, output growth in the Netherlands does not induce employment growth in non-manufacturing.

According to equation (1) the shares of manufacturing and non-manufacturing in non-government output are constant over time, say s_m and s_n respectively. Then it can easily be derived that:

$$p_i = s_n \cdot p_n + s_m \cdot p_m + (s_n - \varepsilon) \cdot (e_n - e_m) \tag{6}$$

holds, where p_i stands for the growth rate of productivity in the non-government sector and ε for the share of employment in the non-manufacturing sector in the total non-government sector. From the discussion of Table 1 we inferred that this share is not constant over time.

---

9. Chatterji and Wickens (1982) also found a good fit for equation (4) of the UK. However, their analysis apparently only holds for that country.

Table 2: Sensitivity of Employment Growth to Output Growth (elasticity of employment with respect to output)

	1962 - 1981				1972 - 1981		
	manufacturing $(1-c_4)$	non-manufacturing $(1-c_6)$	overall weights '62	overall weights '81	manufacturing $(1-c_4)$	non-manufacturing $(1-c_6)$	overall weights '81
USA	0.593	0.190	0.499	0.499	0.549	0.213	0.502
BRD	0.400	0.329	0.467	0.528	0.333	0.328	0.505
UK	0.265	0.284	0.464	0.510	0.284	0.473	0.537
SW	0.371	0.101	0.363	0.491	0.422	0.049	0.486
FR	0.410	0.139	0.358	0.433	0.323	0.250	0.465
NL	0.214	0.423	0.455	0.527	0.018	-0.044	0.246

From equation (6) one sees that non-government productivity growth not only depends on productivity growth both in manufacturing and non-manufacturing - which are explained by equations (3) and (4) respectively - but also on the differences in employment growth in these sectors. The equation illustrates that non-government productivity growth will usually fall short of productivity growth in manufacturing for two reasons. The first is that productivity growth of non-manufacturing is usually lower. The second is that employment is shifted from the manufacturing sector to the non-manufacruting sector (10). A faster growth rate of employment in the latter sector is implied on the one hand by the constancy of shares in value added, cf. equation (1), and on the other by the lower rate of productivity growth in non-manufacturing. This is reflected by substituting equation (1) in equation (6), which yields:

$$p_i = p_m - \varepsilon_n (p_m - p_n) \tag{7}$$

Equation (7) can also be used to derive the impact of output growth on non-government productivity growth. Substitution of equations (3) and (5) yields:

$$p_i = (\varepsilon_m . c_3 + \varepsilon_n . c_5) + (\varepsilon_m . c_4 + \varepsilon_n . c_6) . x \tag{8}$$

which shows that the influences on productivity growth in the different sectors are weighted by their shares in employment when explaining non-government productivity growth. Using equation (8), non-government employment growth, e_i, can be explained from:

$$e_i = -(\varepsilon_m . c_3 + \varepsilon_n . c_5) - \left\{ \varepsilon_m(c_4-1) + \varepsilon_n(c_6-1) \right\} . x \tag{9}$$

Since both c_4 and c_6 will probably not exceed 1, the impact of output growth on employment growth in the non-government sector will probably be positive.

The above discussion of the differences between the manufacturing and the non-manufacturing sectors can now be extended to the differences between the government and the non-government sector. Here the differences are much sharper, since according to equation (2) productivity growth in govern-

---

10. During 1962 - 1981 the per cent increase in ε_n was: USA +0.6, BRD −0.5, UK +4.4, FR −1.5, SW +1.5 and NL +5.1.

ment is zero. As a consequence, we find along the lines of reasoning that led to equation (7) that total productivity growth is explained from:

$$p = \varepsilon_i.p_i \qquad (10)$$

where ε_i stands for the non-government share in employment. From equation (10) one sees that given the rate of productivity growth in the non-government sector, overall productivity growth varies with the share of employment in the non-government sector. Hence the larger the share of employment in government, the lower the rate of productivity growth is in the economy.

However, as a consequence of the above holds that the larger the share of employment in government is, the higher the employment growth, ceteris paribus. This can be seen from substituting equation (1) and (2) in the definition of overall employment growth:

$$e = \varepsilon_i.e_i + \varepsilon_g.x \qquad (11)$$

which shows that the positive impact of output growth on non-government employment growth is enlarged by the positive impact of output growth on employment growth in government. Substitution of equation (9) in equation (11) yields a breakdown of the impact of output growth on employment via manufacturing, non-manufacturing and government respectively:

$$
\begin{aligned}
e = {} & -\varepsilon_m.c_3 + \varepsilon_m.(1-c_4).x && \text{manufacturing} \\
& -\varepsilon_n.c_5 + \varepsilon_n.(1-c_6).x && \text{non-manufacturing} \\
& +\varepsilon_g.x && \text{government} \quad (12)
\end{aligned}
$$

ε_m and ε_n now stand for the shares of employment in manufacturing and non-manufacturing respectively, in total employment. This breakdown can be elaborated using the estimated results presented above.

From equation (12) one sees that the overall impact of output growth on employment growth is represented by:

$$a = \varepsilon_m (1-c_4) + \varepsilon_n (1-c_6) + \varepsilon_g \qquad (13)$$

In effect a is a weighted average of the elasticity of employment with respect to output in manufacturing, $1-c_4$, non-manufacturing, $1-c_6$ and in government where the elasticity is unity. These separate elasticities are summarised in Table 2, together with the overall value. Since the weights in equation (13) will differ from year to year, the overall value of the elasticity of employment with respect to output has been calculated using weights both for 1962 and for 1981. The results are extraordinary. In spite of the difference between the elasticities for manufacturing and non-manufacturing between all countries and the differences between the sectorial shares in employment, the values of the overall elasticities for the different countries turn out to lie very close to each other, in particular when the weights for 1981 are used. The elasticity varies from 0.444 in France to 0.528 in West Germany, when estimated for 1962 - 1981, and from 0.465 in France to 0.537 in both the USA and the UK when estimated for 1972 - 1981. The value of 0.246 for the Netherlands in that period is obviously an exception.

Except for the case of the USA, where the impact within manufacturing is rather high, the overall impact of output growth on employment growth exceeds both that within manufacturing and that within non-manufacturing. As a consequence, the government sector has a positive influence on the impact of output growth on employment growth. Moreover, government has developed in such a way that differences in impact among countries are remarkably small. Actually, we have witnessed during the last two decades a process in which the share of government in value added remained stable over time in all countries, the share of government in employment more or less increased in all countries to the level set by the USA and in which the overall elasticity of employment with respect to output for all countries more or less converged to the level set by the USA of 0.5. As a consequence the elasticity of productivity with respect to output also converged to 0.5. This process occurred in all six countries (except, perhaps, the Netherlands) in spite of their differences with respect to productivity growth, employment growth and government activity.

A final remark should be made on the crucial importance of the assumptions underlying this analysis, represented by the equations (1) - (4). Equation (1) is very important since it implies that the growth in value added of government is equal to the growth in the non-government sector. Next equation (2) states that employment growth in government is equal to growth in value added of that sector and hence equal to the growth in value added of the non-government sector. Equations (3) and (4) establish a rather modest impact of output growth on employment growth via productivity growth in manufacturing and non-manufacturing respectively. However, equations (1) and (2) imply an impact of output growth on employment growth in government of 100 per cent, and hence provide a strong impact of output growth on total employment growth.

The question is, however, whether output growth can be seen as independent of employment growth. In particular, employment growth in government sometimes is said to have a negative impact on output growth. This question is dealt with in the next section.

4. The impact of the welfare state

The modern welfare state is only one of several aspects of the state in developed capitalist economic systems. Other aspects are the industrial state, the scientific state, the military state. It is obvious that these aspects or roles of the modern state will have an impact on the functioning of the economy. This impact, however, is hard to ascertain.

The welfare state is rather a vague concept. This is illustrated by Albeda's (1984, p. 7) definition: "The welfare state is the state that accepts the basic structure of the private enterprise economy; assumes responsibility for the most important macro-economic data (growth of the National Income, employment, income distribution and so on), organises a comprehensive system of social security, etc." The central features of the welfare state are stressed in this definition: government assumes responsibility for a reasonable level of output growth, full employment and a comprehensive system of social security. And having stressed these features, we will not try to give a more specific definition.

In the discussion of the impact of the welfare state on the performance of an economy, both positive and negative influences are mentioned. Labelling these influences in a slightly provocative way, the positive effects can be grouped under the heading 'complements to the market sector' and 'repairshop of the free market system'. One might think, for instance, of:
- the positive influence of a stabilising macro-economic policy compensating shortfalls in effective demand and hence maintaining full employment;
- government regulations coping with external effects of the market sector in the fields of security, health and environmental protection;
- the provision of income transfers and of services such as education and health which are essential for the functioning of a modern economy (11).

The negative influences can be grouped under the heading 'drags on the free market system'. Here one might think of:

---

11. Cf. Maddison (1985).

- the adverse effects on resource allocation of disincentives caused by the tax burden of the welfare state and by petty tutelage of government intervention and regulation;
- biases in expectations with respect to future wages, profits and prices resulting from the anticipation of or real government interference (12).

Both influences are stressed, usually by different authors. However, substantial evidence on the net effect of all influences is hard to find. As Maddison (1985, p. 209) aptly puts it: "It is difficult to reach strong conclusions on the influence of the welfare state on capitalist development because the evidence does not warrant them. Strong judgements on the question are influenced mainly by ideological positions, or predictions about what might happen in the future" (13).

Against this background we are not very embarrassed to admit our disability to cover the wide range of arguments pro and con for the six countries in this study. We can only be very modest in assessing the impact of the welfare state on the economic performance of these countries. Hence, in the line of our analysis above, we will concentrate on the performance with respect to employment growth and productivity growth.

In the previous section we argued that government has a positive influence on the elasticity of employment with respect to output, and hence a negative influence on the elasticity of productivity with respect to output. However, the question remains whether government has a negative influence on output growth. If this is the case, a smaller influence of government may result in, for instance, the same employment growth accompanied by a higher productivity growth. This illustrates the importance of the question.

When discussing the influence of government on output growth, first of all one should comment on the stylised fact that the share of government - including non-marketable services - in value added is constant over time. This suggests a certain complementarity between the market and the non-market sector, which can be interpreted in terms of the 'repairshop' function: the larger the market sector is, the larger is the repairshop which it needs. Moreover, the differences in the shares of government in value added are relatively small over the six coun-

---

12. Cf. Lindbeck (1983) and Calmfors (1983).
13. See also Lindbeck (1981, pp. 60-61) who states: "Unfortunately we do not know much at the present time about the *quantitative* importance of the various above-mentioned effects of the buildup of "high-tax" Welfare States . . . This means that the assessment of the quantitative importance of effects like these is still to a considerable extent an issue of personal judgement in spite of much empirical research in recent years".

tries. As can be seen from Table 1, they do not show any clear relationship with output growth.

However, it is not the share of government in value added on which most studies of the negative influence of government on output growth concentrate. Many disincentives which are said to hamper the working of the free market system, and hence to cause stagnation in output growth, stem from income transfers. For that reason one should look at the share of total public expenditure in national income. Apart from the value added of government, these outlays also include subsidies and income transfers. Data on this share is also presented in Table 1 (14).

As can be seen from the Table, in 1962 these shares were very close to each other for the five European countries, about 35 per cent. In 1982 the shares had increased to just below 50 per cent for the three large European countries and to a level of about 60 per cent for the two small ones. The share of the USA is much lower, it increased from 29 per cent in 1962 to 35 per cent in 1981.

From the data presented in Table 1 it is obvious that there is no clear negative impact of government on productivity performance: nor a high level of the share of government outlays in national income, nor a large increase in this share corresponds to a bad productivity performance. The most outstanding example is the case of the Netherlands, whose productivity performance is almost as good as that of France or West Germany, yet whose share of government expenditure is much higher. Moreover, there is also no clear influence on output growth. This can be seen from Table 3, where a breakdown of productivity growth in output growth and employment growth is presented for 1972 - 1981. We chose the second half of the period under investigation in order to allow for as much influence as possible from divergences in the share of government outlays.

Output growth in the USA, West Germany, France and the Netherlands was 25 per cent over the decade 1972 - 1981, in spite of the different levels of and increases in government expenditure relative to national income in these countries. Output growth in the UK, however, was only 7 per cent, with a moderate position with respect to government outlays. And output growth in Sweden, ranking highest with respect to both its level and its increase in public expenditure, was 17 per cent.

From these figures one might be tempted to conclude that government does not have a hampering effect on output growth. There are two arguments against this conclusion which

---

14. See note 2.

Table 3: A Breakdown of Productivity Growth in Output Growth and Employment Growth for 1972 - 1981 (level of 1981 compared to 1972)

	GNP	Increase in Employ-ment	Product-ivity	Government Outlays National Income
USA '72				32.0
'81	1.25	1.22	1.02	35.4
BRD '72				40.1
'81	1.23	0.98	1.26	49.3
UK '72				40.0
'81	1.07	0.97	1.10	47.3
FR '72				38.3
'81	1.28	1.02	1.25	48.9
SW '72				46.4
'81	1.17	1.08	1.08	65.3
NL '72				48.6
'81	1.27	1.00	1.27	61.5

cannot be refuted, nor corroborated by these figures. The first argument is that the disruption of the structure of the economy is a process which becomes manifest to a notable extent only after a period of more than two decades. A corollary to this argument is that in boom periods the hampering effects of the welfare state are camouflaged. And it is only in the more depressed state of an economy - which also may be partly due to the welfare state - that its hampering effects on the free market system become manifest. However, 1972 - 1981 can hardly be characterised as a boom period. Nonetheless, output growth in the six countries is not visibly affected by the level or increase in government outlays. And it is hard to say what will happen in the long run.

In this context it could also be argued that it is not so much the size but the way of spending public expenditure which will have some effect upon the functioning of the economic system and hence its efficiency. A distinction has been made between the continental pattern of welfare expenditure and the Scandinavian pattern (cf. Kohl, 1983, p. 313), the former being characterised by cash transfers and market reliance while the latter has a preference for public provisions, i.e. non-market transaction. But again, the possible conclusions are not unequivocal. There are good reasons, for instance, to assume that the British public health service is cheaper than the continental (regulated) market system. There are also indications that the Swedish system of public welfare provisions is accompanied by a great deal of government interference with individual decisions causing disincentive effects (cf. Lindbeck, 1981). On the level of our macro data, however, the mentioned distinction shows no correlation with growth differences.

The second argument is that the economic performance of the six countries is influenced by many factors, some of which are general tendencies and some of which are country-specific. One of these general tendencies is the negative influence of the welfare state (and that of strike-happy trade unions perhaps, too). However, for most of the six countries in this study, other influences dominate the negative influence of the welfare state: for instance, the presence of natural gas in the Netherlands and the strong industrial tradition in West Germany. Hence a partial analysis such as ours cannot be conclusive. We agree with that (15). However, even for one country it proves to be very hard to find satisfactory evidence for the assertion that the negative influences of the welfare state are stronger than its positive influences (16). This also reveals a lack of analytical tools in economics. It is a challenge for economic analysis to develop these tools, that is, to develop a model in which both the 'repairshop function' and the 'hampering effects' of the welfare state on the economy are present. To a certain extent the micro foundations discussion is an answer to this challenge. Unfortunately, an answer which is not yet very elaborate.

---

15. However, we recall our conclusion from the previous section that the share of government in employment more or less increased in all countries to the level set by the USA. And due to this process the elasticity of employment with respect to output converged more or less for all countries to the level set by the USA. This process was observed for all six countries in an analysis which was not partial to the extent that three sectors of the economy were distinguished, in an interdependent system. And in this process government provided a positive influence on the impact of output growth on employment growth.

16. See, for instance, Lindbeck (1981, p. 62) who is very careful in stating his conclusions about Sweden.

5. Conclusions

In this paper we tried to analyse the influence of the non-market sector on the development of overall output and productivity in six advanced capitalist countries for the two decades 1962 - 1981. Inspection of the data has revealed two important facts:

- the share of the non-market sector in real output remains fairly constant over time;
- productivity increase in this sector is more or less zero.

Combined with the observation that the output elasticity of productivity growth is positive in the market sector (Verdoorn's Law), this yields two conclusions:

- the share of non-market employment increases with output growth;
- this structural change has a negative effect upon overall productivity growth.

Where growth is constrained by labour supply - as perhaps has been the case in some European countries during the sixties - the government sector clearly decelerates output growth. However, if growth is demand constrained and deficient effective demand brings about a serious threat of unemployment - as was experienced in the whole western world since the seventies - the negative productivity effect of the non-market sector is more interesting because of its equivalent in the sphere of employment. As long as overall output growth remains positive it will have a beneficial employment effect and hence will be stabilising effective demand.

To explain the constant share of government output in real terms we suggest that government services have a supplementary function in overall economic activity. Since they are mainly of a human service character, little rationalisation has been possible, as yet. Hence the zero productivity growth. So it can be said that even within the most developed capitalist countries the market sector is still the leading sector while the non-market sector is a necessary complement and repairshop. To restrict government services in order to improve upon the productivity record would, however, mean jumping to conclusions. Apart from the employment effect, a deficit of government services (education, health, transport, communications, etc.) may cause even more detrimental consequences.

Single country studies very often show much concern about the competitive aspects of the productivity slow-down. One of the more interesting results of our comparative analysis indicates that the share of non-market employment in total employment and the output elasticity of productivity and hence employment growth converge to the level of the most advanced system, the US economy. This result obtains irrespective of differences in employment growth, sectorial productivity growth and government activity. Only the Netherlands seem to be a exception to the rule. We are inclined to conclude from this fact a rather uniform output growth behaviour of advanced capitalist economies despite significant differences in their welfare policies.

This is the last point of interest. Supply side economists accuse the welfare state with its high tax burden of demotivating entrepreneurs, capital savers as well as ordinary workers. It is said to be suffocating productivity and progress. It is difficult to put such an overall verdict to a test, and we do not pretend to be able to confirm or disprove it. Our results, however, allow at least for the conclusion that no corroborative support is given to a supposed negative influence of the welfare state (as measured by the share of government including social security outlays in national income) on either output or productivity growth. Not withstanding their markedly higher welfare activities the European economies seem to have caught up with the advanced US productivity level.

Appendix

Estimated results of equations (3), (4) and (5)

As can be seen from Table A.1, equation (3) provides a satisfactory explanation of productivity growth in the manufacturing sector for all countries in 1962 - 1981. Apart from the USA, for which the fit is rather poor, the determination coefficient is about 0.8 for all countries. In order to see whether effective demand constraints were different in the sixties from the seventies, we also estimated equation (3) for the two subperiods: 1962 - 1971 and 1972 - 1981. As might be expected from the tightness of labour markets in the sixties in most countries, the explanation of productivity growth by equation (3) is better in the seventies - except for West Germany. This is consistent with the results of Wagener and Muysken (1984) (17). Moreover, the values of c_4 estimated for 1962 - 1981 lie remarkably close to those found for 1972 - 1981 for all countries, except for the Netherlands. For that country the value of 0.982 for c_4 implies that output growth in the seventies almost entirely leads to further productivity growth, and hardly leaves any room for employment growth (18). For the other countries c_4 varies between 0.4 for the USA and 0.7 for the UK.

---

17. Compare Wagener and Muysken (1984), Table 2.
18. See also Kuipers, Muysken and Van Sinderen (1978).

Equation (4), on the other hand, poorly explains productivity growth in the non-manufacturing sector: the determination coefficient is about 0.5 for all countries. Therefore we estimated equation (5) directly for all countries using x_n instead of x. Hence we apply Verdoorn's Law also to the non-manufacturing sector. This gives a satisfactory explanation, as can be seen from Table A.2. For both 1962 - 1981 and 1972 - 1981 the determination coefficient varies between 0.7 and 0.8, except for the UK and the Netherlands. For the other countries c_5 varies between 0.7 for West Germany and 0.9 for Sweden in both periods. Since the fit of equation (5) for the UK is very poor, we use for this country the results of equation (4), which are also presented in Table A.2, together with the implied values of c_5 and c_6. For the Netherlands we see again a high value in the seventies for the impact of output on productivity growth. The value even exceeds 1, which implies a negative relationship between output and productivity growth in the non-manufacturing sector.

Table A.1: Estimated Results of Equation (3): $p_m = c_3 + c_4 \cdot x_m$

	1962 - 1981				1962 - 1971				1972 - 1981			
	c_4	c_3	DW	R^2	c_4	c_3	DW	R^2	c_4	c_3	DW	R^2
USA	0.407 (0.112)	0.008	1.95	0.434	0.287 (0.173)	0.017	1.07	0.282	0.451 (0.161)	0.003	2.52	0.496
BRD	0.600 (0.07)	0.019	1.54	0.793	0.542 (0.102)	0.022	1.55	0.801	0.667 (0.139)	0.017	1.30	0.741
UK	0.735 (0.06)	0.013	2.10	0.886	0.807 (0.131)	0.011	1.87	0.844	0.716 (0.091)	0.013	2.04	0.886
SW	0.629 (0.09)	0.014	1.07	0.755	0.282 (0.121)	0.039	1.66	0.475	0.578 (0.122)	0.009	1.18	0.737
FR	0.590 (0.07)	0.018	1.32	0.793	0.457 (0.171)	0.028	1.29	0.507	0.677 (0.119)	0.015	1.11	0.803
NL	0.786 (0.095)	0.017	1.44	0.800	0.676 (0.174)	0.019	0.96	0.684	0.982 (0.132)	0.016	1.63	0.874

Table A.2: Estimated Results of Equation (5): $p_n = c_5 + c_6 \cdot x_n$

	1982 - 1981				1962 - 1971				1972 - 1981			
	c_6	c_5	DW	R^2	c_6	c_5	DW	R^2	c_6	c_5	DW	R^2
USA	-0.015	0.801 (0.138)	1.42	0.670	-0.015	0.882	1.86	0.668	-0.018	0.787 (0.193)	1.40	0.674
BRD	0.016	0.671 (0.119)	1.49	0.650	0.026	0.511 (0.200)	2.15	0.483	0.012	0.672 (0.143)	1.26	0.735
UK	0.011	0.580			0.013	0.523			0.010	0.527		
SW	0.007	0.899 (0.116)	1.93	0.790	0.012	0.789 (0.144)	2.56	0.834	0.004	0.941 (0.203)	2.06	0.729
FR	0.006	0.861 (0.101)	1.96	0.81	-0.008	1.200 (0.227)	1.05	0.800	0.008	0.750 (0.170)	1.94	0.710
NL	0.013	0.587 (0.174)	2.32	0.40	0.024	0.370 (0.344)	2.68	0.142	0.001	1.044 (0.173)	2.77	0.821

* Estimated Results of Equation (4): $p_n = c_0 - c_1 \cdot e_n + c_2 x_m$

	1982 - 1981					1962 - 1971					1972 - 1981				
	c_0	c_1	c_2	DW	R^2	c_0	c_1	c_2	DW	R^2	c_0	c_1	c_2	DW	R^2
UK	0.018	0.694	0.289	1.43	0.45	0.018	0.384	0.340	1.55	0.493	0.016	0.647	0.221	1.12	0.402
		(0.227)(0.09)					(1.197)(0.157)					(0.302)(0.150)			

References

W. Albeda,
The Future of the Welfare State, European Centre for Work and Society, 1984

L. Calmfors (ed.),
Long-run effects of short-run stabilization policy, London, 1983

M. Chatterji and M.R. Wickens,
"Productivity, factor transfers and economic growth in the UK", *Economica*, 1982, pp. 21-38

T.F. Cripps and R.J. Tarling,
Growth in advanced capitalist economies, 1950-1970, Cambridge, 1973

Curzon Price, V.,
"Government intervention as a factor in slower in advanced industrial nations", in: R.C.O. Matthews, ed., *Slower growth in the western world*, London, 1982, pp. 111-121

R. Gerritse,
"Publieke uitgaven en nationaal inkomen: de relatieve ontwikkeling in volumetermen", *Openbare Uitgaven*, 1979, pp. 125-145

J.D. Hilferdink,
"Het reële overheidsaandeel", *Economisch Statistische Berichten*, 1977, pp. 581-583

N. Kaldor,
Causes of the slow rate of economic growth in the United Kingdom, Cambridge, 1966

S.K. Kuipers, J. Muysken and J. van Sinderen,
"De werkgelegenheids ontwikkeling in Nederland sinds 1970: een nadere analyse", *Economisch Statistische Berichten*, 1978, pp. 648-652

J. Kohl,
"Trends and Problems in Postwar Public Expenditure Development in Western Europe and North America", in: P. Flora and A.J. Heidenheimer (eds.), *The Development of Welfare States in Europe and America*, New Brunswick, 1981, pp. 307-344

A. Lindbeck,
"Work disincentives in the welfare state", *National ökonomische Gesellschaft Lectures*, 79-80, 1981

A. Lindbeck,
"The recent slowdown of productivity growth", *Economic Journal*, 1983, pp. 13-35

A. Maddison,
"Marx and Bismarck: Capitalism and Government 1883 - 1983", in: H.-J. Wagener and J.W. Drukker (eds.), *The Economic Law of Motion of Modern Society*, Cambridge, 1985, pp. 197 - 213

H.-J. Wagener and J. Muysken,
"Zur Verlangsamung der dynamischen Effizienz in kapitalistischen und sozialistischen Ländern", in: A. Schüller (ed.), *Wachstumsverlangsamung und Konjukturzyklen in unterschiedlichen Wirtschaftssystemen*, Schriften des Vereins für Socialpolitik NF 142, Berlin, 1984, pp. 117 - 151.

THE IRREVERSIBLE WELFARE STATE

Its Recent Maturation
Its Encounter with the Economic Crisis
Its Future Prospects

Göran Therborn
Joop Roebroek

Rarely in the modern history of advanced capitalism has there been a major institution, which is talked and argued about so much with so little knowledge as the welfare state. Very little is known - in the sense of being digested by prevailing social scientific as well as political knowledge - of the recent developments of the welfare state, of its part in the current international crisis, and, consequently, of the possible futures of the welfare state. Given the severe space and time limits of this article, what will be attempted here can be no more than a modest contribution to some enlightenment of the three problem complexes mentioned.

1. The welfare state in contemporary history

History is the mother and the teacher of the future. Any attempt at an analytical understanding of future options and possibilities, therefore, has to start from the historical grasp of the present. Here, the analysis will be concentrated on two aspects, the location of contemporary welfare states in state history and the socio-economic size and ramifications of current welfare states.

1.1. The silent transformation: the recent arrival of the welfare state

Public social insurance, public health and social care have at least a century-old history. The major international theoretician and architect of public welfare arrangements, William Beveridge, made his epochal contribution in the 1940s, and the accompanying economic theory found its major statement in 1936, with Keynes' *General Theory*. That is common knowledge, but for an understanding of the present - and of the future - it is quite inadequate.

In fact, the welfare state, as we experience it today, is an outcome of the 1960s and the 1970s. In a long time perspective, the extraordinary changes, little theorised and even little noticed, of the sixties and seventies stand out.

Table 1 shows that in the relatively uneventful years of 1960-1982 overall public expenditure grew by an average of 24 per cent in our ten countries. The combined effects of the two World Wars, the 1930s with its, sooner or later, ensuing turn of economic policy orientation (the arrival of Keynesianism) brings an increase of 16 per cent between 1913 and 1949. In the 1950s, during the unprecedented boom, the average increase is 1.4 per cent, as compared with 8.4 per cent in the 1960s, and no less than 14.9 per cent between 1970 and 1982.

In Denmark, Italy, the Netherlands and Switzerland, public expenditure grew more in the 1970s than in the whole period from 1913 to 1960, in Sweden equally as fast. Everywhere, except in Britain, growth in the 1970s is faster than any earlier period of the same length - outside of wartime mobilisation. Inter-state relations of ranking have changed, but inter-state differences have persisted.

No convergent pattern comes out of Table 1.

An idea of the role played by the welfare state in this expansion of the state may be arrived at by looking at the proportion of the former accounted for by expenditure on education, social services, and social transfers (Table 2).

Clearly, the accelerated growth of Western states after 1960 has been mainly due to welfare state growth. In other words, the welfare state has been *the* major factor in the growth of state involvement in the life of the people they govern. No other force is comparable to it.

The rather limited proportion of welfare commitments in the growth of the Danish and Swedish states is most probably in part a statistical artefact, hiding an increase in the number of public employees working in the welfare administrations of the ordinary state apparatus.

This silent change has also meant a major internal transformation of advanced capitalist states. In their everyday activities, Western states have changed from being mainly apparatuses of armed forces, bureaucratic ordering, and of public transport and communication into becoming predominantly institutions of transfer payments to households, of public education and of public caring and public social services. In short, advanced capitalist states have, in their everyday routines, become welfare states. In Belgium and the Netherlands, welfare expenditure in the sense above, amounted to more than half of all public expenditure by 1960 (1). In Sweden this jump occur-

---

1. OECD, "Statistical and Technical Annex", report no. SME/SAIR/SE/83.02, Paris, 1983 (non-published), pp. 42 and 58.

Table 1: Public Expenditure in Some Western European States 1913-1981

Per cent of GDP at current market prices

	1913	1925	1937	1949	1960*	1960*	1970	1982
Belgium	ca 10[1,2]	15/16[1,2,3]	18/19[1,2]	26[1]	35	30	37	57
Denmark	10	13	17	21	24	24	40	61
France	ca 10[2,4]	22	29[5]	37[6]	39	34	39	51
West Germany	17	22	29	31[7]	33	31	39	49
Italy	14[1]	15[1]	26[1]	25[1]	22[1]	30	34	54
Netherlands	8[1]	12[1]	18[1]	27[1]	22[1]	30	46	64
Norway	9[8]	13[9]	17	29	32	26	41	49
Sweden	10	14[10]	17[11]	23	30	31	44	67
Switzerland	14	18[12]	25	20[13]	17	17	21[14]	30[14]
United Kingdom	13	24	25	36	35	33	39	47

* The first 1960 is related to earlier years, the second to later ones.

Notes: 1. Central government expenditure only. Before World War II this limitation of the data had only a marginal effect upon the totals of the countries in question. 2. Estimate form percentage of Net Domestic Product. 3. 1927. 4. 1912. 5. 1938. 6. 1947. 7. 1956. 8. 1910. 9. 1920. 10. 1926. 11. 1936. 12. 1924. 13. 1950. 14. Current disbursements only.

Sources: 1913-1960 First column: Flora, P., (ed), *State, Economy and Society in Western Europe 1815-1975*, Frankfurt am Main, 1983, Ch. 8; 1960: OECD National Accounts, here taken from "Statistical and Technical Annex", report no. SME/SAIR/SE/83.02, Paris, OECD, 1983, non-published; 1970 and 1982: OECD, *Economic Outlook*, no. 35, July 1984, p. 159.

Table 2: Public Outlays on Education, Social Services,
and Social Security 1960 - 1981

Per cent of the Gross Domestic Product. Current prices

	1960	1981	Per cent of public expenditure increase 1960-1981
Belgium	17	38[1]	95
Denmark[2]	10	29	53
France[2]	13	24	73
West Germany	20	31	65
Italy	16	29	81
Netherlands	16	36	105
Norway	12	27	68
Sweden[3]	15	33	55
Switzerland	8	15[4]	78
United Kingdom	14	25	85

Notes: 1. 1980. 2. Exclusive of education. 3. Exclusive of other social transfers than social insurance, family benefits and social assistance. 4. 1979.

Source: Calculations from: OECD National Accounts, here taken from "Statistical and Technical Annex", report no. SME/SAIR/SE/ 83. 02, Paris, OECD, 1983, non-published.

red between 1966 and 1968 (2). By 1981, all advanced capitalist states, even the USA and Japan, devoted more than half of their public expenditures to welfare state purposes (3). With regard to terms of public employment, in the Scandinavian states employees in education, health care and social care now comprise between 2/3 and 3/4 of all public employment (4).

---

2. Calculated from: Forsman, A., En teori om staten och de offentliga utgifterna, Uppsala, 1980, p. 133, and: OECD, National Accounts, 1963-1980, Paris, 1982, p. 209.
3. OECD, "Statistical and Technical Annex", op. cit., pp. 30-69.
4. 62% in Sweden in 1981, 68% in Denmark in 1981, 76% in Norway in 1980. All figures exclude employees in public enterprises operating on competitive markets. Calculations from: Nordisk Ministerrad, Den offentliga sektorns sysselsättningsutveckling i Norden under 1970-talet, Oslo 1983, p. 6.

In the Netherlands in 1977 about 57% of all government and government-subsidised para-statal personnel were occupied with teaching, caring, and other social and medical services (5). In brief, Western states have largely become post-bureaucratic welfare states.

1.2. The socio-economic ramifications of the welfare state

Above we have seen that the contemporary welfare state is not an elderly institution, susceptible to the ailings of old age. On the contrary, the developed welfare state is a very recent phenomenon, better characterised by the, sometimes extravagant, vitality of youth. In our time, the welfare state has also become a major institution of advanced capitalist societies. One expression thereof is the significance of the welfare state as a source of income.

Thus, as Table 3 shows, between one fifth (Japan) and one third (Netherlands and Sweden) of the sum of household income derives directly from the state.

Calculated in terms of income recipients, the significance of the welfare state is even greater. By the late 1970s, old age pensioners and public employees together make up more than half of the voting-age population in Britain and Sweden, and close to half in West Germany. In the USA public employees plus recipients of social security and of social assistance constitute about 35% of the adult US population in 1975 (6).

In the Netherlands, old age pensioners and public employees are not so numerous - roughly 30% of the electorate in 1981 (7).

---

5. *De kwartaire sector in de jaren tachtig*, The Hague, 1980, pp. 147 and 241. From the total of the 'quartery sector', private practitioners of medicine, dentistry, and physiotherapy as well as personnel in private childcare have been excluded.

6. Calculated from: Rose, R., "Changes in Public Employment", Centre for the Study of Public Policy, University of Strathclyde, Glasgow, 1980, p. 91.

7. Public employees from: Ministerie van Binnenlandse Zaken/ Sociaal en Curtureel Planbureau, *Over voorzieningengebruik en personeel in de kwartaire sector 1983-1987*, The Hague, 1983, pp. 14, 67, 69, 71 and 77. Doctors, dentists, and physiotherapists have been excluded (as private practitioners). Population and electorate from: CBS, *Statistisch Zakboek 1982*, The Hague, 1982, pp. 23 and 75. Since public and para-statal employment is statistically given in man/years, the proportion of the electorate is only a rough indicator (the exact percentage from this estimate was 29).

Table 3: Sources of Household Income in Selected OECD Countries as a Percentage of Current Receipts in 1980

	Income from Public Employment*	Social Security**	Entrepreneurial/ Property Income
United States	13[1]	12	17
Japan	8[2]	12	25
France	12	24	20
West Germany	14[2]	18[2]	22[2]
Italy	10[3]	17	28
Netherlands	12[1][9]	25	16
Sweden	22[12]	21	10
United Kingdom	16	12	16

*   For the United States, Japan and Italy, for which direct data are not available in international reference works, public employment income has been estimated by substracting 'intermediate consumption' from 'government final consumption expenditure', although some operational costs will thereby be included. Double counting in the case of Sweden and the Netherlands may exaggerate the true figure by 1 per cent. All data is calculated from the cost perspective of the employer, thus including social security contributions. The latter are of major importance in Sweden and France, of medium significance in the Netherlands, Italy and West Germany, of minor significance in the US, UK and Japan. The Dutch and Swedish figures in parentheses refer to public wages and salaries without employers' contributions. The compensation of employees of public corporations is not included.
** Social Insurance, social assistance, and 'unfunded employee benefits'.

Notes: 1. 1978. 2. 1979. 3. 1976.

Sources: Calculated from: OECD, *National Accounts 1961-1980*, Paris, 1982, Vol. II, national tables 8 and annex 1; income from public employment in France and West Germany calculated from: IMF, *Government Finance Statistics Yearbook 1982*, Washington D.C., 1982; British, Dutch and Swedish wages and salaries from national sources: *Social Trends*, no. 13, London, HMSO, 1982, p. 88; CBS, *Nationale Rekeningen*, The Hague, 1983, p. 118; *Arbetsmarknadsstatistisk Arsbok 1982-1983*, Stockholm, SOS, 1983, pp. 158 and 163.

On the other hand, given the massive failure of Dutch capitalism to provide employment, the total number people receiving their main income from the state is huge. In 1983, 49% of all income recipients below the general pension age of 65 received their income from the welfare state, 27% as receivers of social benefits and 22% as public or parapublic employees (8).

2. The welfare state and the economic crisis

The current, ten year old international economic crisis has, of course, affected the parameters of the welfare state. However, from the earlier discrepancy between the dramatic growth to maturity of the welfare state and, on the other hand, the relative lack of attention to and comprehension of it, we should rather expect another gap between real developments and the foci of prevailing public discours. The latter is, in fact, the case.

Ideologically and politically, the welfare state is currently under heavy attack. This phenomenon is most briefly summarised in the election of the militantly right-wing liberal regimes of Thatcher and Reagan, seconded by several other governments, most wholeheartedly by the Lubbers Cabinet in the Netherlands and in retreating positions of the Mitterand government, the US Democrats, the Dutch, and the Danish Social Democrats, and the disarray of the British Labour Party. In social science, the way the wind is currently blowing is most directly felt from the strongly increased influence and assertiveness of anti-Keynesian economics. But major social institutions can hardly be knocked down by rhetoric alone, or from electoral platforms or academic chairs. Let us take a look at a few facts about actual developments.

2.1. The effect of the welfare state upon the economic crisis

Developed capitalist welfare states remain subordinated to the business cycles and the structural crises of the international capitalist economy. The current crisis has shown that generous systems of social security in themselves provide no security against unemployment. But anti-welfare statists cannot have Standardised rate of unemployment as per cent of the labour force in the fourth quarter of 1983. Average annual growth of GDP 1978-1983, in per cent. Public expenditure for health, social and welfare services (transfers, public consumption, capital expenditure exclusive education) as per cent of GDP in current prices in 1981

---

8. Centraal Planbureau, *Centraal Economisch Plan 1984*, The Hague, 1984, p. 320.

Table 4: Unemployment, Economic Growth, and Social Expenditure[1]

	Unemployment	Economic Growth	Social Expenditure
Australia	9.5	1.8	12.8[2]
Austria	4.2[3]	1.8	24.1
Belgium	14.9	1.5	32.6[2]
Canada	11.1	1.6	15.5
Denmark	(10.6)[4]	1.6	29.0
Finland	6.2	3.8	23.3[3]
France	8.2	1.8	23.8
West Germany	7.8	1.5	26.4
Italy	10.0	2.1	22.7
Japan	2.6	4.3	12.5
Netherlands	14.0	0.7	29.1
Norway	2.8	2.5	21.0
Sweden	3.4	1.5	(31.9)[5]
Switzerland	(0.4)[6]	1.5	9.4[7]
United Kingdom	13.1	1.1	19.0
United States	8.4	1.8	15.0

Correlations: Spearman's rank order correlation (8)
between unemployment and economic growth: r = −0.50;
between unemployment and social expenditure: r = 0.35;
between economic growth and social expenditure: r = −0.34.

Notes:

1. The country set is exhaustive of all advanced capitalist countries, except the smallest ones of Iceland and Luxembourg; New Zealand has been left out for lack of reliable unemployment data.

2. 1980.

3. Third quarter of 1983.

4. Non-Standardised rate for 1983.

5. The original data source had no final consumption and capital expenditure for social and welfare services. The latter have been assumed to be of the size of that of Denmark in relation to social transfer payments. This will be seen as a conservative estimate.

6. Non-standardised rate for 1982.

7. 1979.

8. Due to the less than perfect comparability of the data, differences in the unemployment rate of 0.5% or less and of social expenditure of 1% or less have been left out. But as the Swedish figure is lower in 1980 than in 1981, Belgium alone is highest in social expenditure.

Sources: Unemployment: Denmark: Det Okonomiske Rad, *Dansk Okonomi December 1983*, Copenhage, Direktoratet for Statens Indkob, 1983, p. 52; Switzerland: *OECD Observer*, no. 127 (March 1984); the rest: OECD *Quarterly Labour Force Statistics 1984*, Paris,

1984, p. 76. Growth: 1982-1983, *OECD Observer* no. 127, 1978-1981, OECD, *Economic Outlook*, no. 33 (July 1983), p. 160; Social expenditure: OECD, "Statistical and Technical Annex", report no. SME/ SAIR/SE/ 83.02, Paris, 1983, non-published, pp. 31-69.

their grain ground here; there is no inverse relationship between social policy extension and unemployment. The evidence is contradictory.

Economic growth has become a weak predictor of unemployment, only a fourth of the variation in unemployment at the end of 1983 can be accounted for by the economic growth between 1978 and 1983 ($r^2 = 0.25$). Between the size of social expenditure - from which education has been excluded here in order to accentuate the more controversial social security aspect - and low unemployment there is a small negative relationship ($r^2 = 0.11$) as well as between social expenditure and economic growth ($r^2 = 0.12$). In other words, only one ninth and one eighth respectively of variations in unemployment and of economic growth may be statistically accounted for by the extension of public social commitments.

Briefly and crudely summarising a long argument (9) contrary to the McCracken Report (10) and other conventional wisdom, states can maintain a low level of unemployment even in the face of a deep international crisis, provided there is a deeply institutionalised commitment to high employment. But general Keynesian demand management is not enough, a compatible monetary policy and/or an extensive selective labour market policy is also required. Non-market control over employment is crucial, whether through extensive public works and retraining as in Sweden, public subsidies as in Norway, public industrial employment as in Austria, publicly supported paternalism as in Japan or public control of immigration in an immigrantdependent economy such as that of Switzerland.

Combining the extension of social security commitments and an institutionalised full employment commitment, the following typology of welfare states can be arrived at with regard to both employment and social security.

The trichotomy of social security commitments has been guided by a search for significant break-points, such that the distance between the lowest scoring country of one group and

---

9. The argument is developed and sustained empirically at some length in a forthcoming book: Therborn, G., *Why Some Peoples Are More Unemployed Than Others*, London, 1985, forthcoming.

10. McCracken, P. (et al.), *Towards Full Employment and Price Stability*, Paris, 1977.

the highest scoring of the next group below should be larger
that the distance between the former and the second lowest
country of the country of the same group.

Commitments to social security and commitments to full
employment thus vary independently of each other, something
which has to be brought into the centre of the welfare debate

Diagram 1: A Typology of Contemporary Welfare States

Full Employment Commitment

	Institutionalised	*Non-Institutionalised*
Social Security Commitment		
Major	Sweden	Belgium Denmark Netherlands
Medium	Austria Norway	Finland France West Germany Italy United Kingdom
Minor	Japan Switzerland	Australia Canada United States

Sources: Table 4 (social expenditure) and the analysis of
economic and labour market policies undertaken and elaborated in: Therborn, G., *Why Some Peoples Are More Unemployed Than Others*, op cit.

and analysis (11). We may give our typologised countries de-
scriptive labels.

1. The Strong Welfare State (Sweden), highly committed to
   social security and capable of preventing mass unemployment even in the face of a deep worldwide economic crisis
   and with a low rate of national economic growth.
2. The Soft Welfare State (Belgium, Denmark, Netherlands),
   gene rously committed to social security, but unable to control their labour market.

---

11. Manfred Schmidt has been a pioneer in this respect. See his
"Arbeitslosigkeit und Vollbeschäftigungspolitik", in: *Leviathan*, no.
4, 1983. Our analysis and evaluation are not quite the same as his, however.

3. The Full Employment Oriented Medium Welfare States (Austria, Norway), giving priority to employment policy.

4. The States of Socio-Economic Mediocrity (Finland, France, Germany, Italy, United Kingdom), distinguishing themselves neither in social nor in employment policy.

5. The Full Employment Oriented Market States (Japan, Switzerland), dedicated to maintaining full employment but with limited commitments to social security.

6. The Market Oriented States (Australia, Canada, United States), where, in spite of significant welfare state developments in the short run the market is unequivocally given the upper hand, in income as well as in employment determination.

The world of advanced capitalism is a world of wide variations in public and in individual life-chances.

2.2. The real impact of the crisis

Table 5 shows that the average annual growth in social security expenditure declines in almost all Western countries under review (except France) between 1975 and 1981. However, until 1982, social security expenditure continues to grow at a respectable pace. There are considerable annual variations but with the exception of Australia and Canada in 1979 (and also New Zealand in 1980), there has been no absolute decline in any country, although there has been for individual programmes, most often in family benefits. (12)

For developments after 1981 we will have to resort to national data of various kinds. The Reagan administration has concentrated its cuts on means-tested programmes for the poor, but social security (old age, disability, and survivors) benefits grew in real terms by 15% between 1980 and 1983, and hospital insurance (for the aged) by 25% (13). In Britain under Thatcher, public expenditures on social security grew from £25.336 million in the fiscal year of 1978/79 (under Labour) to £28.444 million (in 1978 prices) in the fiscal year of 1982/83 (14). In the Netherlands, net public transfers to households

---

12. See OECD, "Statistical and Technical Annex", report no. SME/SAIR/SE 83.02, Paris, 1983, non-published.

13. OECD Economic Surveys 1983-84, *United States*, Paris, December 1983, p. 15. For an interesting and informative overview of Reagan's budget and social policy see the interview with budget chief David Stockman, in: *Fortune*, February 6, 1984, pp. 35.

14. Social expenditure in current prices from: Central Statistical Office, *Social Trends*, no. 13, London, 1983, p.90. Consumer Prices Deflator from: OECD, *Economic Outlook*, July 1984, p. 161.

(net of insurance premia paid) have grown from an average of 3.3% of national income in 1976-1980 and 4.6% in 1981 (when the Social Democrats took part in the government) to 5.0% in 1984, exclusive of the growth caused by the rise in unemployment (and in unemployment compensation) (15).

*Table 5: The Annual Growth in Expenditure on
Social Security*

In percentages, 1970 constant prices

	1965-70	1970-75	1975-81
Australia	5.0	15.4	2.5[2]
Austria	5.8	5.5	4.8
Belgium	8.7	9.6	5.5[2]
Canada	12.1	12.1	3.3
Denmark	10.0	5.8	4.3
Finland	11.3	10.0	5.1[2]
France	8.0	6.3	7.6
West Germany	5.7	8.0	2.1
Italy	7.8	8.1	3.3
Japan	13.8	11.9	8.7
Netherlands	12.7	5.6	4.6
Norway	13.3	7.0	6.3
Sweden	10.9	9.7	4.6
Switzerland	8.9	10.4	2.7[1]
United Kingdom	5.8	6.0	5.1
United States	9.7	9.3	3.1
Average	9.3	8.8	4.6

* Expenditure on health, temporary sickness, pensions, unemployment, family benefits and other transfers.
Notes: 1. 1975-1979. 2. 1975-1980.
Source: Calculations from: OECD, "Statistical and Technical Annex", report no. SME/SAIR/SE 83.02, Paris, 1983, non-published.

---

15. Centraal Planbureau, *Centraal Economisch Plan 1984*, op. cit., p. 157.

But figures do not always tell the whole truth. Welfare state expenditure is still growing, but this is not to deny that painful cuts and redistribution measures from labour to capital and from the poor to the well-to-do are being made by governments, and not only by right-wing liberal regimes, but also by coalition governments with social democratic participation. The measures are nearly the same in most Western countries: (a) changes in indexation of benefits, implying less than full compensation of price increases; (b) more strict entitlements to benefits, such as in unemployment insurance, and taxed paid services; (c) certain tendencies towards privatisation: relatively more beds in private hospitals compared with public hospitals; public controlled services, especially in the health service sector, are accommodated to the private sector; (d) a tendency towards de-individualisation of rights of social insurance and re-strengthening of the 'breadwinner' principle in entitlements to social insurance; (e) rationalisations, especially in the health services; (f) shifting costs: less redistribution over the public budget and more emphasis on direct payments for services and insurance premia. In Belgium, the Netherlands, and the United Kingdom these measures are accompanied by a discussion about a more fundamental reapraisal of the system of social security on the base of actions taken by the government.

With regard to the welfare state as a whole, the real impact of crisis policies have so far been marginal and, more, unable to break the trend of growth. But it is worthwhile to investigate whether these policies reveal recent changes in political power relations.

2.3. The welfare state and political power relations

The explosive growth of the welfare state in the sixties and early seventies is on the political plane accompanied by a strengthening of the position of labour vis-à-vis capital. That is the effect of wide-ranging social processes that undermine patriarchy and the family control over production, challenge clientelist and religious forms of social control of production and class division, increase the scarcity of labour on the market, and diminish the dependence of those who are not owner-occupiers upon the labour market for their support (16). This development results in a compromise of the main political actors, wherein the welfare state provisions occupy an important place.

---

16. See: Therborn, G., "The Prospects of Labour and the Transformation of Advanced Capitalism", in: *New Left Review*, no. 145, May/June 1984, p. 37.

What happened to the political power relations from 1975 on? In most countries the crisis policies cracked the existing compromise. To answer the question more carefully, a more thorough analysis of government social policy in the crisis has been made for a group of Western European countries (17). As a first result, two diagrams are presented: one contains an overview of the point of time that a 'crisis statement' is given, the 'first significant cuts' are carried out and the discussion about a more fundamental reappraisal of an important part of the welfare state, the system of social security, starts; the other reveals the composition of the government at these moments.

A first conclusion that can be drawn is that at the time of a 'crisis statement' (and also of the 'first significant cuts') with one or two exceptions (Netherlands and Sweden) the social democrats form a coalition government (in Belgium with the confessional and liberal parties) or take in a dominant position within the government. Secondly, a discussion about a more fundamental reappraisal of the system of social security and the launching of plans in that direction exclusively takes place under right-wing governments. In the two countries where the discussion is advanced and the governments proposed plans for the reappraisal, the right is relatively better represented in the governments that announces the 'crisis statement' and carries through the first 'significant cuts'. In two countries in which the discussion is started by conservatives and liberals, Denmark and the United Kingdom, social democracy is defeated in an election after a long period of governmental power and sent back to opposition.

These developments indicate that under the surface of a relatively unbroken growth in the welfare state a change in the political power relations has taken place. A development that needs some more attention with regard to the future of the welfare state.

This shift in the power relations should not be understood as an exclusive effect of changes in electoral favour. It is a more structural development not only of social and political relations, but also of social and political moods. It is a field of forces in which political parties, labour unions, employers organisations, and others try to influence decisions that are made within government, parliament, and other organs. In this field one

17. The analysis is based on materials from the project "The Political Future of Social Security: Political Demands and Social Relations of Force". This project is financed by the 'Commission for Research on Social Security' (COSZ) of the Dutch Ministry of Social Affairs and Employment.

can, in general, distinguish three positions with regard to the welfare state: on the one side the organisations and forces which advocate a more selective orientation (privatisation, restriction of rights, stricter rules for adjudication of benefits) and on the other hand the organisations and forces which stand for a more solidary orientation (maintenance, and where necessary a further extention of provisions). This differentiation is characterised by a third position, a strengthening of the centre position. That is a 'no stalemate' situation, in the sense that political

Diagram 2: The Policy of Welfare: a Sequence of Actions

	Crisis State-ment*	First Significant Cuts**	Fundamental Reappraisal***
Austria	1983	–	–
Belgium	1976	1980	1983
Denmark	1980	1980	–
France	1982	–	–
West Germany	1975	1977	–
Netherlands	1978	1980	1983
Sweden	1982[1]	–	–
United Kingdom	1976	1977	1983

(1)   In Sweden the 'Crisis statement' was made by the incumbent bourgeois government in the winter of 1982. After the re election into office of the social democrats in September 1982, the social cuts that accompanied the 'crisis statement' were redrawn and did not take effect.

*   'Crisis Statement' refers to the moment that the government announces that the policy of welfare can not be continued without changes.

**   As criterion for 'first significant cuts' we use three standards; firstly two quantitative ones: is there an annual growth in expenditure on social security of less than 2 percent and/or does a decline in the annual growth of more than 3 percent appear; besides that a qualitative one: are the changes in a more quantitative sense the result of obvious alterations in policy? This estimation is based on materials until 1982.

***   'Fundamental reappraisal' refers to the statement by which the government takes the initiative for a possible fundamental change in the social security system as a whole. Usually this is done through the setting up of a public commission of investi gation with far-reaching tasks.

Diagram 3: The Policy of Welfare and the
Composition of the Government*

	Crisis Statement	First Significant Cuts	Fundamental Reappraisal
Austria	left	–	–
Belgium	coalition	coalition	–
Denmark	left	left	right
France	left	–	–
West Germany	left	left	–
Netherlands	right	right	right
Sweden	right	–	–
United Kingdom	left	left	right

* Here we used a threefold distinction: 'right' (conservative-liberal-confessional), 'coalition' (social democracy in a balanced coalition with one of the right-wing parties) and 'left' (a government dominated by social democracy).

manoeuvring is blocked. This situation has its own dynamics, based on an internal logic: solutions are sought in the direction of a reduction in social expenditure and cuts in welfare provisions, without exceeding the general framework of the existing arrangements and leaving the general objectives of the welfare state untouched.

In terms of political actors the first position is mainly composed of the conservative, liberal, and larger or smaller parts of confessional parties, the employers organisations, and sometimes middle-class organisations; the other is made up of the social democratic, communist, and other progressive parties, the labour unions, and organisations of consumers of services and recipients of benefits. The strengthening of the centre is usually the result of a move to the centre of parts of the christian democratic party and/or parts of the social democratic parties.

The development in power relations since 1976 indicates a shift in the direction of domination by the position with more solidary to the position with a more selective orientation.

Generally we can conclude that the resistance to significant changes within the welfare state, even in a situation wherein a domination of the selective orientation exists, is so strong, that until now a fundamental reconstruction of the welfare state is excluded. Even in the Netherlands, it is not obvious that the defeat of the trade unions in December 1983 weakens the position of the political actors with a more solidary orientation to such

Diagram 4: Changes in Power Relations Between a More Solidary and a More Selective Orientation

	Domination Solidary Orientation	Centre Position	Domination Selective Orientation
Austria	1975-1982	1983-now	
Belgium		1975-now	
Denmark	1975-1980	1980-1982	1983-now
France	1975-1982	1982-now	
West Germany	1975-1977	1977-now	
Netherlands	1975-1977	1977-1982	1982-now
Sweden	1975-1981 1982-now	1982	
United Kingdom	1975-1976	1976-1979	1979-now

* This overview has been made on the base of electoral results, changes in the composition of governments, actions to economise, and the results of confrontation between both positions.

an extent that the announced reconstruction of the social security system will be carried through entirely.

3. The future of the welfare state

Basically, on the basis of the evidence given above in section 1.2. and further sustained by the record summarised in part 2.1., we hold that the welfare state is an irreversible major institution of advanced capitalist countries. Or, to be more precise, it is irreversible by democratic means. The size of the population benefiting from the welfare state ensures that as long as democracy accompanies advanced capitalism, the core of the welfare state is safe. This goes against a great deal of hopes on the right and fears of the left. But it is not enough. We have seen above that the welfare state is a variable, not a fixed entity, and an assessment of its possible future will have to pay attention to possible variations. Our general analytical perspective involves two fundamental causes of welfare developments: socio-economic tendencies and socio-political power relations.

3.1. Socio-economic thrust

The major push ahead of the welfare state is the ageing of the population of advanced capitalist countries, except Belgium (18). This ageing of the population stands not only for more pensions and more old age services. It also means a great increase in health care. For the Netherlands, it has been calculated that between 1981 and 2000 a growth in expenditure (for pension benefits, nursing homes, old people's homes, old people's welfare work and medicines) of more than 20% is needed to maintain existing standards (19).

Another push of welfare state expenditure derives from unemployment. Currently, almost all predictions point to an enduring rate of massive unemployment among two thirds of advanced capitalist countries, which fails since 1975-76 to maintain full employment. This means the establishment of a virtually permanent pool of unemployed. Except in Belgium existing unemployment insurance is not geared to handling long-term and permanent unemployment. Under existing political conditions permanent mass unemployment is likely to produce mounting pressure for economic provision for the long-term unemployed at a level above that of social assistance.

A third major upward pressure on public social commitments may be expected from population concerns. In most Western European countries, the current rate of reproduction is negative, and it may be expected that procreation-stimulating social policies will be adopted. In Sweden, this is already a consensual issue.

Forthly, the number of single mothers is likely to increase. Particularly in countries with high unemployment and current low rates of females labour force participation, this implies an increasing demand for social assistance.

The visible tendency of expenditure on public education to decline significantly alleviates the pressure, due to demografic changes in Western populations. For the Netherlands, this means a possible declining in expenditure between 1981 and 2000 of 20% maintaining the existing level of education (20).

3.2. Fiscal constraints

The fiscal constraints of social policy are not absolute facts. They are to a large extent politically defined and affected by

---

18. OECD, "Statistical and Technical Annex", op. cit., pp. 94-108.
19. Sociaal en Cultureel Planbureau, *Collectieve uitgaven en demografische ontwikkeling*, Rijswijk, 1984.
20. Sociaal en Cultureel Planbureau, *Collectieve uitgaven en demografische ontwikkeling*, op. cit., p. 86.

policy outcomes. The enduring crisis does not mean a permanent depression, as the current upturn shows, in which a growth rate of 2.5% in 1984 is forecast for the European Community and of 4.5% for the OECD as a whole (21). A calculation by the OECD Secretariat for the seven major Western countries estimates that, due to declining needs for education expenditure, a constant GDP share of welfare state expenditure could ensure a 0.7% annual growth rate in real social benefits until 1990 (22). On the whole, there seems to be little reason for doubt that the current level of social welfare commitments, or even a moderately higher one, is payable.

However, there are at least two qualifications to be made here. Pension insurance schemes in many countries are very sensitive to lower rates of growth and/or high rates of unemployment. In some countries revisions have already been made, and further ones are not unlikely.

Secondly, some countries have already incurred large financial deficits in the public sector. The mounting interest burden of this debt and the narrowed policy margins of big structural deficits is most likely to constrain future social policy. This holds, above all, for Italy and Belgium, but also, to a lesser extent, for Denmark, the Netherlands, Canada, and Sweden (23).

3.3. Socio-political forces of welfare state demands and defence

At least one major social force behind the welfare state is growing and is likely to become more active and demanding in the future. That is old people, the 'senior citizens'. They are growing in numbers, and they are becoming more vital and active, due to the combination of increased longevity and reduced retirement age. The aged are also by far the most important beneficiaries of the welfare state. Pensions and health care of the aged make up the bulk of social security expenditure in all countries. As the French specialist Anne-Marie Guillemard has said: "The welfare state is, first and foremost, a 'welfare state-for-the-aged'." (24). The demands of the aged are likely to grow for social, cultural, and recreational services, and they are likely to be vigilant with regard to their pension rights and levels.

---

21. Centraal Planbureau, *Centraal Economisch Plan 1984*, op. cit., p. 19.

22. OECD, *Social Expenditures 1960-1990*, Paris, 1985.

23. The size of general government financial deficits is given in: OECD, *Economic Outlook*, July 1984, p. 27.

24. Guillemard, A.M., *Old Age and the Welfare State*, London, 1983, p. 97.

Another interested welfare state defender is the group of welfare state employees. Their number is unlikely to grow in the near future, but it is quite significant already, between a fourth (in Sweden) and a tenth (the USA, West Germany, and Italy) of the economically active population (25). This is a well organised and highly articulate category of people.

Welfare state employment has been especially important for the emancipation of women, who usually occupy the major part of that kind of jobs. Large-scale attacks on the welfare state are therefore likely to meet with resistance from articulate women, even outside welfare state employment.

Finally, the labour movement, in modern times the major political protagonist of the welfare state. In the countries with high unemployment, it is currently being weakened, and tendencies to a division between private and public employees are appearing. However, even after some recent setbacks, the labour movement in most advanced capitalist states is located on a historical high plateau of strength and acquired rights (26).

3.4. Pre-conditions for right-wing retrenchment

Above we have given a number of reasons for our conviction that the welfare state is irreversible by democratic means, and also for our belief that in the foreseeable future even successful cuts and restrictions will not change the fundamental base of it. However, countries vary in their line-up for and against the existing welfare state, and further variation cannot be excluded. On the contrary, there are strong grounds to expect a further divergence among advanced capitalist states over the coming five to ten years. This derives above all from the divergent impact of the current economic crisis, in particular with regard to unemployment. The enormous differences in the rate of unemployment, shown in Table 4 above, are likely to have an enduring, diverging impact for two reasons. First, all OECD estimates indicate that these differences will remain for the rest of the 1980s (27). Secondly, and also partly an explanation for the former, contrary to pre-crisis predictions or fears, mass un-

---

25. Calculated from: Rose, R., *Understanding Big Government*, London, 1984, pp. 132 and 139.
26. See further: Therborn, G., "The Prospects of Labour and the Transformation of Advanced Capitalism", op. cit.
27. Whether mass unemployment will remain a feature of some advanced capitalist countries throughout the 1990s is a question which we do not feel competent to answer here. But we do regard the total rejection of this possibility by the authors of the ILO report *Into the twenty-first century: The development of social security*, Geneva, 1984, pp. 11 and 102, as irresponsibly sanguine.

employment has not led to massive socio-political upheaval. Mass unemployment Netherlands remains as calm as low unemployment Sweden.

Before going further, however, a major qualification has to be made. Politics and policy are not amenable to scientific prediction. Rather than expecting their specific predictions to come true, political scientists would do well to adopt as a major law of politics the title of a book of short stories by Andre Maurois, *Toujours l'inattendu arrive* (the unexpected always happens).

We should thus formulate our predictions as conditionals, 'if a, then (probably) b'.

The fundamental precondition for a significant right-wing dismantling of the welfare state is a division, a demoralisation, a decomposition, and finally, an at least partial political marginalisation of the broad coalition of socio-political forces which supported and sustained the welfare state expansion in the 1960s and 1970s. The building of a socially majoritarian anti-welfare state coalition, dedicated to capital accumulation and to private business ideology seems impossible in the foreseeable future. The best evidence for the latter assertion is given by the comparative class analysis of Erik Olin Wright. Wright combines the scientific commitment of Althusserian Marxism with post-orthodox theoretical sophistication and the large-scale empirical surveys of American Big Science. His results indicate that even in the United States, about 60% of the labour force have at least a minimum of pro-labour or working-class consciousness. In Sweden the corresponding figure is 90% (28).

Then, what are the preconditions for a division, demoralisation, decomposition and partial marginalisation of the welfare coalition? First, high unemployment and/or other kinds of worsening in the condition of labour, incurred under a government in which the major left-of-centre party takes a significant part. The record of the successful low unemployment countries strongly suggests that such a major policy failure is not due, primarily, to the openness to and the force of the international economic system, but to half-hearted, contradictory or adverse policies. The electoral defeats of the British Labour Party (in 1979), the US Democrats (in 1980), the Danish Social Democrats in 1982, and the Dutch centre-left in 1982 fit into

---

28. Wright, E.O., "What Is Middle about Middle Class?", in: *Prokla*, 1985, forthcoming, tables 2 and 5. Cf. further: Wright, E.O., *Classes. Theoretical and Empirical Problems in Marxist Class Analysis*, London, 1985, forthcoming.

this pattern, as does the current defensive attitude of the Mitterand regime.

However, the original division and demoralisation of the forces of the left and the centre-left have to be reproduced for the right to be able to make significant inroads into the welfare state. For this reproduction there are a number of possibilities, not mutually exclusive.

Second on our list, as the strongest and most reliable of the mechanisms of reproducing left division, demoralisation and decomposition, is a dualistic socio-economic development. A dualistic economy and society - of a dynamic, well-off sector and a stagnating or declining sector of low-wage or unemployed misery - is the medium term goal of the new right, consciously or unconsciously. And the fact is that some advanced capitalist societies are beginning to take on those features, earlier held to be characteristics of Third World societies only. Thus, in Britain, an increase in unemployment from 5% in 1979 to 12% in 1982 was accompanied by a slight increase in consumer expenditure, measured in constant prices (29). The US economy grew by 7.6% between June 30 1983 and June 30 1984, but unemployment was still 7.1% at the latter date (30). The more a dualistic economy and society is created, the stronger the dismantling pressure on the welfare state. The current upturn in the international business cycle is likely to produce significant dualistic effects even in societies and politics not so extreme as the American and British ones. The economy is also beginning to grow again in Belgium, Canada, Denmark, and the Netherlands, but mass unemployment - and the misery of the unemployed - remains.

Managing a dualistic economy and society by democratic means is largely dependent, however, on the character of the political system. This is our third variable, the more elitist the political system, the easier a right-wing attack on the welfare state. One important measure of elitism is the prevailing electoral turnout. In this respect, Western democracies currently fall into three groups. 1. The Exclusive Democracies: Switzerland and the United States, with an electoral turnout at around 50% of eligible voters; 2. The Reduced Participation Democracies, with a 70-85% participation rate: the United Kingdom, Japan, the Netherlands, Finland, Denmark, Nor-

29. *Economic Trends*, London, Central Statistical Office, March 1983, pp. 10 and 36.
30. *The Economist*, 28.7 - 3.8.1984, p. 83.

way; 3. The Full Participation Democracies: the rest (31). Elitist politics, reinforced by the first-past-the-post electoral system, means that Thatcher and Reagan were elected into office by less than a third of the electorate.

Finally, there are policies reproducing left-wing defeat. We began our list of variables conducive to right-wing attacks on the welfare state by indicating the fateful effects of anything less than whole-hearted commitment to full employment in the period of 1975-1982. We will end it by listing a set of policies most likely to ensure the reproduction of the dominance of the right. From the point of view of the latter, the policies may be read as targets.

(a) Disunity between trade unions and the political parties representing labour. The greater the disunity, the greater the chances of a right-wing retrenchment. This is both a question of institutional structure - the extent of the elitist middle class character of the party, thereby starkly distinguished from the unions. The American, British, Dutch, and French cases indicate this. But it is also something affected by policy, as the "Shulterschluss" between the Social Demoratic Party and the unions in West Germany after the eviction of the Schmidt government exemplifies.

(b) Concessions from a weak position in the hope of reciprocity. "Givebacks" of collectively bargained wages and other benefits in a weakened position are likely to produce mainly internal division and demoralisation, and unlikely to bring forth equivalent concessions from the counterpart. This tactic has been pursued by some American unions - that of the steelworkers above all - and, en mass, by the Dutch unions, seconded by the Dutch Labour Party. The main effect of this is likely to be a strengthening of the self-confidence and the assertiveness of the political right and of the employers. The West German unions and Social Democrats have, after losing office, opted for another tactic. The result of the latter is more respect for the concerns of labour.

(c) Selective social policies. There is a dilemma in social policy between general and selective policies. In order to be overall effective and truly general, the former have to be high in transfer payment and in quality of services. This makes them very costly and also tends to reduce their redistributive effects. On the other hand, selective services tend to be, or become, of

---

31. European Management Forum, *Report on International Industrial Competitiveness 1984*, Geneva, 1984, table 10.03. French figure corrected with regard to presidential election of 1981.

lower quality, and selective social policies are or become very vulnerable to political attacks, since the set of beneficiaries is restricted. Therefore, the more selective, geared only to the poorest, social transfers and social services are, the more likely they will be subject to retrenchment attempts. Thus, to the extent that left-of-centre parties and trade unions adopt selective social policies, e.g., in the form of 'basis' services and transfers plus optional superstructures, the more likely the level of the 'basic' provisions will become the object of attack.

(d) Decentralised labour policies. The strength of the labour movement, and of the welfare coalition as a whole, rests on its numbers and its unity. To the extent that policies are adopted which are not based on those assets, the right and the anti-welfare state coalition will gain. This implies that the more collective bargaining is decentralised, the more specificities of private and public sectors, industrial branches, and enterprises are opted for in the current period, the stronger the position of capital, and of the anti-welfare state forces.

4. Brief conclusion

The welfare state has become a major and (by democratic means) irreversible feature of advanced capitalist societies. The current welfare state crisis discussion is little more than an ideological fad, which serious researchers cannot take seriously. On the other hand, a divergence of Western welfare states is likely to take place in the foreseeable future. The failure to maintain full employment from 1975 is likely to have enduring effects. Furthermore, the reactions to the earlier failures diverge. The West German labour movement seems to have learnt from its past, whereas in, for example, the Netherlands, strong left-of-centre forces appear heading for further defeats.

However, we would rather end by saying that the future remains open. As political human beings, we are committed to full employment and to social security. And it is our hope to have contributed to clarifying the path to be taken for such a future.

THE CONSERVATIVE CRITIQUE OF THE WELFARE STATE AND THE PROBLEM OF DEMOCRACY

David Plotke

If this conference were occurring ten or fifteen years ago, discussion might centre on expanding and democratising the social policies of the welfare state. Criticism might claim that these policies were insufficient, and that the gap remained great between stated objectives and actual accomplishments. Some might argue that the proliferation of new programmes did not mean an expansion of services, but an elaboration of new categories for old problems. The welfare and social policies of the 1960s might also be criticised as politically demobilising. Constituencies activated by state promises and organised social movements were divided and bureaucratised, narrowing the scope of reforms while deflecting deeper political challenges (Piven and Cloward 1971). The premise of this imaginary discussion would be that the welfare state is here to stay. We would then discuss whether its expansion would be sufficient to meet new needs, and democratic enough to sustain political participation.

Today the context for discussing social policy and the welfare state is very different. In the United States, and also in Great Britain, Canada and elsewhere, the consensus on expanding welfare social policies has broken apart. While some core programmes have been retained under the Thatcher and Reagan administations, other programmes have been curtailed or eliminated. Both governments oppose most new social policy and welfare initiatives. Thus today the problems of the welfare state are not only problems of administration or funding, but also political problems, sometimes extending to its premises.

I will first sketch the conservative critique, and then indicate possible responses. The second part of the paper will analyse the prospects of the conservative critique, in policy and political terms, and propose an alternative course. This approach takes seriously a central conservative accomplishment. Conservatives have argued that social policy matters very much for economic growth, mainly by blocking or distorting it. They have rejected the dominant post-war conceptions, in which growth was assumed and social policy was conceived either as a distribution of a surplus, or, at some economic junctures, as a secondary means of sustaining aggregate demand. I will agree that social policy matters, but argue that post-industrial forms require expanded social policy initiatives to yield sustained socio-economic development compatible with democratic principles.

The conservative critique of the welfare state has become a popular, electorally successful critique in the U.S. and elsewhere (Burnham 1982; Therborn 1984). Social and economic circumstances have encouraged this outcome. Slow and erratic economic growth has segmented the population in new ways, breaking linkages among the lower middle class, working class, and poor, linkages which facilitated electoral support for welfare state measures. Slow growth has also encouraged the view that welfare expenditure comes at the expense of investment; thus they hinder development which might raise the general standard of living.

Politically, the critique of the welfare state has been encouraged by the evident intervention of the state into new areas of social life. State intervention has been criticised as a bureaucratic and intrusive effort to impose the cultural values of the cosmopolitan upper middle classes. This critique does name aspects of the experience of the lower middle and working classes in several countries.

While these developments may have opened the way for a conservative critique of the welfare state, they did not guarantee its success. The latter has required sustained political and theoretical argument against what only recently was the political common sense of the dominant forces in the U.S. and elsewhere.

The conservative critique

The assault on social welfare policies comes from several sources in the United States: the traditional conservative right; virtually the entire Republican Party, which has shifted to the right over the last decade; the new right, a collection of groups motivated by cultural conservatism and conservative economic populism (Crawford 1980; Whitaker 1982); and neoconservatism, the opposition by many liberals of the 1960s to social policy measures with an actively interventionist scope and egalitarian aims (Steinfels 1979). These forces are not always unified. Neoconservatives, for example, support most pre-Great Society welfare policies, but criticise many policy efforts after the mid-1960s, while some traditional conservatives have never really accepted the welfare policies instituted in the U.S. in the 1930s and 1940s.

Here it is important to distinguish the situation in the United States from that of Canada, and more sharply from that of

Britain. There are many ways of defining the welfare state. A policy definition might include a state commitment to provide insurance against personal risks (health or accident-related); to maintain income (unemployment insurance, pensions); to provide supplementary income (family allowances, etc.); and to eliminate poverty through establishing a minimum income. A more modest definition, framed in terms of state functions, might define the welfare state as one committed to cushioning the effects of the market on the population of advanced capitalist countries: providing a significant measure of income redistribution; aiming at full employment; involving diverse social groups in negotiating policies; and developing a state apparatus to implement the above policies.

The United States does not meet either set of criteria, while Canada comes much closer, and Britain, prior to Thatcher, met most of them. For the U.S. it is more accurate to talk about welfare policies than presume that the situation is essentially similar to that of Western Europe. The principle of national health insurance - much less a nationalised health system - is not accepted in the U.S. A redistributive conception of welfare policies was not solidly accepted, even prior to Reagan, as emergency and charity models of public assistance remain influential. In the United States the attack on welfarism has taken shape as an attack on a welfare state which has been only partially realised. Nevertheless, the critique of welfare social policies has included economic, political, social, and moral themes.

The economic critique of welfare policy has charged social policy expenditure with encouraging growing deficits and inflation. This argument does not accept that such measures compensate for their deficit-creating short-term consequences through maintaining demand.

An economic critique also claims that government intervention creates unexpected economic consequences which interfere with market operations. Such interference involves inefficiencies which slow growth; thus a short-term transfer of resources is counterbalanced by a long-term reduction in welfare even for the direct beneficiaries of welfare policies (Friedman 1983; Sowell 1980).

The political critique of welfarist social policy has attacked the addition of layers of bureaucracy to the national state and to state and local governments. These policies have been expensive to fund and administer. Perhaps more important, welfare state policies have spurred the growth of clientelistic networks around the state. As interest groups press claims for greater benefits, elected officials have great difficulty in resisting such claims, and their weakness creates an upward budgetary spiral. Welfare statism leads to a stagnant, rigid policy which is neither governable nor particularly democratic.

This view of welfare policies appears prominently in neoconservative critiques which stress that the state's decision-making capacities have been weakened. The result is not more democracy, but less, as bureaucratic politics and interest group manoeuvering (usually accompanied by populist rhetoric) restrict effective governance (Huntington 1981).

A social critique of welfare policies has charged their proponents with refusing to examine the real policy consequences. This critique emerged in the 1960s, with Daniel Moynihan's criticism of anti-poverty and community action programmes in the Johnson administration (Moynihan 1969). He argued that claims to create democratic community involvement masked the advancement of narrow social interests. Some welfare recipients established privileged clientelistic positions, and professionals treated an expanded social policy apparatus as a chance for personal and political advancement.

Welfare social policies have also been attacked as disrupting communities. In the name of equality and assistance to the needy, the state intervenes without sensitivity to communal forms, to mediating institutions between the state and the individual (Berger and Neuhaus 1977). The result is that any positive consequences of the effort are annulled by the disadvantages of disrupting communities which provide various forms of moral and material support. Democratic schemes do not yield democratic results simply through good intentions.

Finally, moral arguments have been made against welfarist social policy, warning about the dangers of statism and the weakening of individual responsibility. Conservatives and neoconservatives claim that welfarist social policies substitute state initiatives for those of private citizens and associations. The quality and variety of social life decline, as people look to the state to solve problems which they ought to consider within their own competence. Statism undermines the moral requirements of a free and healthy society.

This moral critique sometimes centres on the effects of welfare policies on clients who come to depend upon the state for their very survival. Welfare services encourage dependency; rewards for individual initiative decline, as do penalties for personal and familial irresponsibility (Gilder 1981).

Neoconservatives affirm the need to sustain many of the policies established in the 1930s, which taken together cannot be called a welfare state in the U.S., but do outline a minimal framework of social protection. They are joined by conservatives who accept the need for (conservative) welfare policies (Will 1983). Some conservatives, however, reject philosophically most arguments in favour of any government welfare policies; and in policy terms, seem unreconciled to the accomplishments of the 1930s.

The more extreme position has converged in practice with the neoconservative critique around a programme which calls for at least reducing the growth of social policy expenditure, and cutting back programmes; privatising services; and reducing popular expectations. The latter point is stressed as a way of breaking with a welfarist model, in which proliferating interest groups can press demands which taken together are totally unrealistic.

In the United States, the limit of the practical critique of welfare policy is the notion of a "safety net" to catch those who have been unable to support themselves. The moral dimension of the argument emphasises that individuals are responsible for avoiding dependence on the state. Thus state policies should not aim at the goals of the welfare state - eliminating poverty, ensuring employment, redistributing income, providing insurance, etc. Instead, state policies should help individuals recover from private disasters where necessary, prevent utter degradation among people genuinely incapable of self-disciplined advance, and provide a framework which rewards individual enterprise.

There is a tension between the conservative commitment to the market and economic development and the valorisation of the communal and traditional against the state. Yet the conservative critique has taken shape as a powerful claim both to economic efficiency and to moral virtue. The attack on welfarist social policy has not been framed as a simple matter of self-interest. (Nor has it appeared in explicitly racial terms, despite racial undertones.)

Two responses to the conservative critique have thus proven inadequate in the U.S. and elsewhere. One argument tries to unmask conservative policies as benefiting narrow groups (Piven and Cloward 1982). This is problematic when those who reject welfarism insist that in the medium-term the results will benefit everyone. A second approach cites evidence or examples of harsh results of social policy restrictions and cutbacks, which have not been lacking under Reagan or Thatcher. Yet these episodes do not invalidate an argument about medium-term necessities, and the appeal to misery also faces the claim that welfarist social policy has not reduced misery.

If pointing out the immediate human costs of the assault on welfare policies is insufficient, it is still important. Yet a response to the attack on welfare social policies must confront the main themes of that critique. The conservative argument has insisted on linking economic and social policy. In the U.S., it was believed that Keynesian economic policies could yield sustained economic growth; in this setting, social policy could cope with secondary (even if large) problems. In the United States, the objects of social policy have been defined as marginal problems in the sense that their resolution does not involve reshaping economic policy or the economic order. The focus instead is on preparing disadvantaged groups and individuals to participate more effectively.

The conservative critique rejects a separation between economic and social policy, and the notion that social policy can assume growth. This critique insists that welfarist social policy influences growth - negatively. Growth is jeopardised, directly through the costs imposed by welfare policies, and indirectly by economically inefficient political processes. The conservative critique claims that social policies have been morally destructive of the discipline and initiative required for sustained economic growth in market societies.

Responding to the conservative critique

The conservative critique has gained ground over the last decade in the U.S., Canada, and Britain, with different emphases in each country. In the U.S. the attack on welfare policies has been linked to two other positions. First, there is a critique of positive state intervention in the racial order, via affirmative action or similar programmes, as unfair, destructive of individual effort and disruptive of community (Glazer 1976). Second, there is an attack on state regulatory policy, especially environmental regulation, for impeding investment and growth (Pertschuk 1982; Kristol 1978).

In Great Britain, the critique of welfare policies has more often focused on the power of trade unions. This has led to an attack on corporatist conceptions of political decision-making. In the United States such an attack would be misplaced. Truly corporatist forms are even more underdeveloped than the welfare state, due to the weakness of the labour movement, the decentralised federal political structure, and proliferating interest groups and social movements which decline the mediation of either the labour movement or business elites (Salisbury 1979). Despite these different situations, one can pose general elements of a response to the conservative critique.

A response to the conservative economic critique must acknowledge that inflationary aspects of social policy spending cannot be wished away. As well, social policy measures can help place pressure on profits which may threaten the willingness of business to invest productively.

Yet an economic distinction can be made between the core social programmes (such as social security and unemployment insurance), mainly established in the 1930s in the U.S., and most other programmes, especially the novel forms of the 1960s. The former play a majole in the budget. The latter played a modest role even before the Reagan budgets (Bawden and Palmer 1984). Eliminating them altogether would not have major economic consequences. Nor would modest cuts in the core entitlement programmes. Reducing government welfare expenditure enough to make a major budgetary difference would probably mean slashing the "safety net" conservatives claim to support. Posed this way, the issue divides those who are committed to at least minimal welfare policies from those who are not.

What about a profit squeeze created by welfare policies and government regulation? Profits did decline in the U.S. in the 1970s, and an increased social wage and regulatory pressure played a role.

The real question is whether adequate funds exist for new investment. If they are not on hand, would cutting welfare policies and regulatory requirements create them? This question depends essentially on what business elites deem a reasonable rate of profit. Across nations no necessary relationship exists between the profit rate and the rate of investment. Nor is there a simple positive or negative relationship between state social spending and economic growth.

The notion of a zero-sum situation in which profits fall due to increased wages (bolstered by the social wage) or regulatory costs attributes too much rationality to the customary operation of markets in the U.S. Perhaps a hydraulic relationship would exist if the entire economic mechanism were taut, with no wasted resources, underutilised skills, or ineffective forms of management. This is very far from the situation. New investment funds are actually and potentially available without slashing federal spending on welfare policies; whether they are mobilised is partly a political and social question (Bowles, Gordon, and Weisskopf 1983).

The conservative political critique of welfarist social policy is not unfamiliar to the latter's defenders. The new programmes were sometimes badly bureaucratic, and sometimes intrusive. Yet the conservative argument is inconsistent. The programmes are blamed for being costly, bureaucratic, and inaccessible; they are also blamed for making the state too accessible to interest group pressure.

The conservative critique would not have gained the ground it has without corresponding in some measure to popular experiences of the state. Yet one can still take issue with the substance of the conservative position. It is not true that the more innovative social policy measures were as responsible for the organisational expansion of the state as is often claimed. New social policies were often implemented through a redivision of the state with modest expansionary consequences.

But how would cutting back new and old social policies improve the political situation? Quasi-welfare policies would be left to local elites, inside and outside of government. There might be a renewal of patronage systems which have never been known for their efficiency. These forms would be less democratic than the bureaucratic institutions whose procedures are at least indirectly open to public debate. Here the conservative critique is an abstract and moralistic critique of flawed institutions which have usually been more democratic than those they supplemented or displaced.

To the conservative political argument that social policy has increased political fragmentation by empowering interest groups, a fuller response is necessary. Social policy in the 1960s and 1970s often did activate new movements and interest groups. Yet how would governance improve if the groups encouraged by welfarist social policies were weakened?

Some bureaucratic elements of welfarist social policies deserve criticism, but the modest ways in which they encouraged popular mobilisation in the U.S. deserve support. The political problem in this country is not a hypermobilisation but an extraordinary public apathy toward politics, reflected in voting rates lower than those of virtually any other Western country. The problems of interest group competition for resources are not due to welfare state policies so much as to a conservative involution of the electoral universe. Were political participation to increase dramatically, the problems of interest group competition might diminish through a logic of electoral competition and reorganisation. The threat to democratic institutions in the U.S. comes more from popular political withdrawal than from the mobilisation encouraged by welfare state policies.

The conservative social critique also needs a sharp response. The concern for unintended consequences is a basic conservative argument which always has some merit. All social action creates unpredicted effects. Yet welfarist social policies have been forms of rational social action. They have failed at times, but their failures have not been simply irrational, and alongside the unintended consequences there have been significant intended accomplishments.

The conservative assault on social policy often amounts to a repudiation of deliberate social reform in favour of (at most) cautious institutional adjustment. This stance understates the costs of existing arrangements, while cultivating sensitivity to costs which might result from changes. This argument can defend the claims of order, but is not intrinsically persuasive about the meaning of social policies.

As well, the claim that recent welfarist policy innovations mainly expanded job opportunities for professionals is only a partial truth. New social policy initiatives created a demand for professionals. But it is reductive to disqualify these policies on such grounds. Whether or not professional positions have increased, welfare policies should be judged by their broad political and social effects. To reduce this judgement to a hostile treatment of new professional strata cynically simplifies, while making a quasi-populist claim to protect "the people" against state interference.

Yet the conservative social critique's communitarian emphasis deserves careful attention. Welfare and related social policies have disrupted communities. They have sometimes taken statist forms, confusing and even enraging some of the people the programmes were meant to serve. The alternative, however, was usually a reliance on the market which would have been at least as disruptive. Here a basic tension appears. The conservative critique of welfare policy valorises community ties, mediating institutions, and free associations of citizens. At the same time, it claims to defend the market against political intervention. Some conservatives try to bridge this tension by claiming both the market and community as spheres of freedom and individual initiative. Yet market forces undermine the communities and linkages which conservatives value. Unregulated market-based growth would (and does) rapidly consume non-market social forms. A response to the conservative critique can acknowledge that welfare policies can be destructive - but refuse to accept that relying on the market will be more respectful of communal ties.

Finally, the moral arguments against welfarist social policy make legitimate claims. Welfare policies may create new dependent relationships and then reinforce them. Statism can lead to passivity. (It was not always conservatives who made similar critiques in the 1960s!)

Yet the state policy initiatives of the last two decades rarely replaced lively democratic forms in the United States. More often, they replaced market relations, or personalistic and clientelistic social forms. The latter had some virtues, even dignity. But they were often both frankly undemocratic and inefficient in providing services.

The forms of dependency associated with new welfare policies have rarely been worse than prior forms of dependency. Welfare recipients can now make political claims which they could not easily make before; this is an increase in political participation, not simply increasing dependence. Here the conservative antagonism towards interest group pressure on the state has an anti-democratic cast.

These points sketch the direction of a response to the conservative assault on welfare social policies. Such a response should acknowledge problems with these policies, yet insist that the situation would not be improved by further reducing welfare provisions in a country in which they have been very modest. Such a course would not create public virtue and private discipline, but limit the practical possibility of democratising new and old social policy institutions. Even a generous recognition of the merit of the conservative critique should not obscure two points: welfare spending is not the central cause of the economic difficulties of the last decade; and without welfare measures, democratic values would be weakened.

Prospects for the conservative project

The conservative critique has gained and sustained wide popular appeal in the U.S., Canada, and Great Britain. In the United States, the election and re-election of the Reagan administration have permitted a conservative critique to be expressed in policy choices. Even if Reagan had been defeated, a Mondale administration would have had no chance of returning to Democratic welfare and social policies of the 1960s. In Canada, the Conservative Party's course promises a similar though more moderate approach than that of the Reagan administration. In Great Britain Thatcher has won two elections in which the conservative critique of the welfare state has been a major theme of her campaigns.

The electoral successes of conservative administrations do not necessarily ratify the conservative critique of the welfare state. Public opinion polling suggests an attachment to specific existing programmes, along with hostility to social spending. (Such hostility is greater among men than women in the U.S., and much greater among whites than blacks.) This pattern of opinion helps to protect core programmes, but also legitimates cutting back the programmes of the 1960s, as well as blocking the introduction of major new programmes.

The political appeal of the conservative critique of the welfare state in the U.S. has relied on the themes outlined above. An anti-statist populism has claimed to represent hard-working, productive citizens against unreasonable tax burdens (Phillips 1982). Measured by the criteria of conservative theorists, the political shift has not been great enough, and the need to reduce welfare spending remains. Compared to routine shifts of opinion in mass democratic politics, the conservative critique has been very successful in shifting the terms of political debate in the last decade in the U.S. The question of how welfare and social programmes might best be developed and improved has become the question of how they might best be trimmed. (Part of this shift has involved the identification of social welfare programmes, in the broad sense, with "welfare" as the delivery of services and income to particularly disadvantaged subpopulations. The result is that the stigma attached to the latter in popular political debate is diffusely linked to many social policies.) Major political figures are reluctant to take initiatives towards an expansion of welfare policies. This is a striking success.

How has the conservative critique been expressed in policy measures? As is typical in American politics, the major shifts were achieved early in Reagan's first term (when the political capital of the incoming administration is generally greatest). The overall direction has remained steady since then.

Reagan's policies have had three main dimensions. First, there has been a sustained effort to limit the growth of spending on "core" entitlement programmes, primarily social security. Where this has been most politically controversial, Reagan has sought a bipartisan consensus, partly to gain immediate support, and partly to protect his efforts from subsequent electoral attacks. The growth in spending in these areas has been slowed (Nathan 1983). At the same time, Reagan's success has exposed a division within the conservative coalition, between those who are really committed to sustaining the core programmes, and those who want to cut them back radically.

Second, the Reagan administration has sought to weaken or even eliminate many of the welfare and social policy programmes initiated in the 1960s and early 1970s. This has often been attempted through administrative strategies rather than a frontal legislative assault (Bawden and Palmer 1974).

Third, the growth in new programmes has been arrested. This dynamic continued past the 1960s, even through the Nixon administrations. While new programmatic demands continue to emerge, there is little likelihood that a second Reagan administration will initiate new programmes (Glazer 1984).

However one judges the merits of this programme, by American standards there has been considerable success in putting it into effect. Questions concern the political and economic consequences of the conservative programme. Politically, the immediate effects have been uncertain. Reagan's most supportive constituencies have been pleased with the changes. Yet in general, rather than reinvigorating the public spirit, the conservative programme has encouraged apathy or less often a countermobilisation. Rather than taming interest group competition, there has been a shift in which groups have most access to power. Yet Reagan's anti-statism remains popular, so that these negative political consequences do not disqualify it from electoral success.

At the economic level, it would be hard to make a serious argument that cuts in welfare programmes have had much of a positive effect on the overall economic situation. It might be argued that they have prevented a bad budget deficit from being worse. But the significant economic growth - following a severe recession - of Reagan's first term has stemmed more from deficit spending than budget-cutting.

Along with his tax policies, Reagan's social policy cuts have encouraged a regressive income redistribution. This has not been as dramatic as some of Reagan's critics have claimed; combined with real economic growth, it has meant an absolute increase in family income for most Americans. But both the absolute and relative income shares of the bottom fifth of the population have fallen (Moon and Sawhill 1984).

Perhaps cuts in government regulations have had some effect on raising productivity and encouraging investment, but if so, it is probably a one-time effect. The sources of growth lie mainly in the expansion of new sectors where government regulation is not a crucial problem, and less in the reduction of regulation within older industrial sectors.

In the short-term, Reagan's conservative programme has been relatively successful in its own terms. One should not underestimate the political appeal of this programme, even apart from its immediate socio-economic effects. In Britain, where Thatcher's first government was much less economically successful than Reagan's, re-election was still possible. In the United States, the popular perception of an improved and improving economic situation certainly helped Reagan. If he had been defeated, there would have been no electoral mandate for a major expansion in welfare spending.

Thus there is now a stalemate. While the conservative assault has been so successful that many of its objectives have been gained, those who wish to entirely dismantle the American quasi-welfare state will find themselves blocked not only within the governing coalition but by opposed forces, in the Democratic Party and organised interest groups. On the other side, proponents of expansion and innovation in social/welfare policies have been unable to win their argument. In the theoretical debates, conservative arguments have had considerable success, and the practical problems confronting Keynesian policies have made conservative theories seem more compelling.

In this context, proponents of almost any version of a welfarestate face a slow but profound erosion of the programmes they would defend unless they can ground their proposals without relying on the renewal of central economic institutions in their post-war forms. Many defenders of the welfare state have despaired of any such effort. They have abandoned much of the terrain to conservatives, while fighting on narrowly drawn questions of programme efficiency or trying to make new austerity as humane as possible.

Democracy and development in social policy

The conservative case rejects much of welfarist social policy and valorises the market. A reinvigoration of the market requires complementary social policy measures, reducing intrusions in and alternatives to market sources of sevices and support. In the conservative argument, welfare and other social policies represent a deduction from possible investment. This view is increasingly shared across the political spectrum. Many liberals who oppose specific programmatic cuts believe that slow economic growth requires austere welfare policies (the current position of much of the Democratic Party). And some neo-Marxists frame this problem as a conflict between accumulation and legitimation (Offe 1984). If this consensus is accepted, then debate shifts to how extensive cuts should be and how they should be administered.

There is evidence for this counter-position of investment and other social spending, though much of it is indirect. Keynesian policies which used to work seem not to have been working over the last decade, or at least not working well enough to survive politically.

Yet what if the assumption of a choice between accumulation and social welfare is not correct, at least in the broad form in which it now justifies assaults on welfarist policy? While opposing the two is correct for some areas and some programmes, the argument is incorrect as a medium-term prognosis. It confuses the decline of the post-war model of accumulation with contemporary possibilities. Keynesian models of economic intervention have not stopped working because some fixed limit to state expenditure has been reached. Rather, the economic institutions which underpinned Keynesian policies have been decaying in the advanced countries (Block 1984). From the 1930s to the 1960s, Keynesian policy could stimulate mass production industries. Their expansion created increased employment, stimulating further demand, which would eventually reduce deficits. Elements of this pattern remain in the current American expansion.

In the 1980s, the post-war mass production industries no longer occupy the same central position within the economy, either in terms of output or employment. Keynesian stimuli still create additional demand, but that does not create much additional employment in the traditional industries, as new technologies increasingly replace labour, and more flexible production systems are introduced. Thus Keynesian policies are unlikely to lead to sufficient new employment; unemployment rates drift upward along with welfare demands (Bell and Kristol 1981). On the other hand, a pure market strategy will not solve employment problems, as evidenced by the aspects of the current American experience, in which social and regional inequities deepen in a wild process of economic and social modernisation.

While the decay of post-war industrial forms is underway, new socioeconomic possibilities are emerging. The latter may make it possible to ground a new conception of the role of welfare and social policy. The outlines of a new economic model indicate that its most dynamic sectors are in computers, electronics, and related activities, as industries in their own right and as sources of industrial transformation throughout the economy. In this model, growth depends on scientific and technical inputs. New investment is labour saving and even capital saving. Service work grows both at the top and the bottom of occupational hierarchies.

This economic transition allows - and may require - linking welfare expenditure to a positive model of economic and social development. Thus social policy and welfare policies in particular have new rationales which are both urgent and broad.

The basic point is that most existing and much new welfare and social spending is economically efficient for societies whose development requires an expansion of scientific and human service activities, while labour time in direct goods production is declining. Such societies require a skilled, flexible population capable of learning and relearning. Careers will lead in and out of the formal labour market, educational institutions, and families. The adjudication of claims to paid employment will be a critical political and social issue.

In this context, social policies are necessary not only for job training in a narrow sense. They are also crucial for developing learning capacities, and for assisting individuals in transition between the formal labour market and other activities. The relevant programmes may often redraw the line between "welfare" policies (in the narrow sense of that term in the U.S.), and broader social policy expenditure. Bridging this gap may provide an opening for rebuilding political linkages among the lower middle class, the working class, and the underclass, linkages which have weakened and sometimes snapped over the last fifteen years.

In the short term, it is impossible - and morally deficient - to insist that every welfare expenditure conform to a criterion of medium-term economic rationality. Many severe immediate problems, which existed prior to the current administration but have been intensified by its policies, demand urgent attention on grounds of equity and decency. Some such problems concern racial inequalities, while others involve what has come to be known as the "feminisation of poverty" (Ehrenreich and Piven 1984). Aside from the moral demands that these problems make, policies to address them do have substantial elements of medium-term economic rationality. In general, the vast costs of the transition to "post-industrial" socio-economic institutions involve massive externalities of the sort which all but the most extreme free market ideologists recognise in principle. These costs occur in old and new areas, both where older communities are devastated, and in newly booming areas, where wild growth spawns serious problems, from environmental disasters to family violence.

Arguing that socio-economic change requires new social policy interventions does not mean that all such efforts should be conducted through the state. One can imagine, for example, that retraining programmes would not be based simply on expanding state educational institutions, but involve a combination of improved state facilities and voucher mechanisms which individuals could employ in public or private settings.

Old and new unemployment problems

I have argued for the "post-industrial" economic rationality of social policy and welfare expenditure in very general terms. Here I will briefly discuss one issue in more detail.

In the United States, unemployment provides an important representative example. In the post-war period it was assumed that Keynesian policies could reduce unemployment to socially acceptable levels. The central role of mass production industries made this approach viable, as a general economic stimulus

would quickly reach these industries. Their expanded employment and production would have significant multiplier effects
across the economy; and the stable employment of male heads
of household would help support families. In this context, the
role of social policy was to even out market imbalances with
selective labour policies; job training policies, for example,
would attempt to involve limited groups who suffered from regional or sectorial shifts. Welfare policies coped with extremely
disadvantaged individuals and those unable to enter the labour
market.

The decline and internal transformation of the mass production industries, coupled with the expansion and differentiation
of new sectors, changes the above dynamics. Keynesian stimuli
do not reinstate historic levels of employment in the mass production industries. It is not possible to find a single sector with
the centrality for both production and employment across the
entire economy of the post-war automobile industry. Claims to
paid employment rise - especially but not only by women. Thus
official rates of unemployment rise from one cycle to the next,
while the "potential" rate of unemployment - the rate which
would exist if all those with a serious interest in paid employment were actively looking - rises steadily.

In this new setting, social policy cannot possibly cope with
unemployment and underemployment problems if it proceeds
with the conceptions and resources appropriate to a setting of 3-
5% unemployment, and relatively low levels of "potential" unemployment. Social policy must be concerned with the effects
of growing unemployment and underemployment on entire
groups, communities, and regions.

The boundary between social policy labour market approaches and welfare policies becomes less clear, inasmuch as
the objects of both policies face similar problems. Unemployed
steelworkers in 1984 present very different problems than did
unemployed steelworkers in 1964. For the latter, unemployment was viewed (often rightly) as a temporary condition to be
dealt with by macro-economic policies which by stimulating the
economy would increase the demand for steel and thus bring
these workers back to the factories. Today such displaced
workers will for the most part not be recalled to work by a general economic expansion. Without easily transferable skills,
they have much in common with some groups of welfare recipients and marginal workers, regarding both their needs and
prospects.

In this setting, a broadened social policy, integrated with expanded welfare policies, should be concerned with the effects
of growing unemployment and underemployment on entire

communities, regions, and categories of actual and potential employees. Anything less is, in economic terms, a massively inefficient approach to human capital issues. Social policy would then become an important component of active efforts to shape socio-economic life. Such efforts will of course be resisted, especially when they constrain market operations, or help reshape relations among family and work across life cycles, or defend the claims of disadvantaged groups to paid employment.

In sum, unemployment is an issue for which the main postwar Keynesian approaches are no longer adequate. In practice, efforts to apply these approaches can fuel conservative rebellion against deficits and inflation. Yet a broad economic rationality does not lie in scrapping social and welfare policy, but in restructuring and expanding both to address the emerging problems of the present transition.

Funding and organisation

Yet even making a persuasive case for the economic rationality of welfare expenditure will be politically insufficient in the present context, unless new initiatives are made regarding financing and organisation.

First, the financing of welfare and social expenditure must avoid relying on relatively regressive taxes on the lower middle and upper working classes. This reliance often helped shatter liberal and social democratic coalitions in the last fifteen years (Sears and Citrin 1982). Without restructuring tax policy, new political coalitions in favour of social spending will be very difficult to sustain. Such policies face constraints, and it is demagogic to claim that sufficient funds can be obtained by soaking the rich. The crucial political criterion is that tax policies be seen as fair and as reasonably related to general social purposes, rather than being seen as unfair burdens placed on the marginally fortunate to sponsor narrow groups among the less fortunate.

Second, the problems of democracy and paternalism must be addressed regarding the organisation and delivery of welfare state programmes. There are no panaceas in this area. But as the 1984 election campaign suggests, there remains great popular resentment of "the state" and of "special interests" which are viewed as aiming to capture privileged positions near the budgetary process. The following criteria are intended to outline features of proposed new programmes, and of reorganisation efforts of existing programmes.

Programmes should be clear, with explicit statements of objectives accessible to the public and participants.

Programmes should be as simple as possible, with easily understood regulations governing the relation of programme activities to programme goals.

Programmes should be developmental, that is, they should enable those involved to expand their participation in social life.

Programmes should be flexible and interactive, allowing scope for local and regional adaptation and for participants to shape elements of their participation.

Programmes should be unifying. They should bridge current divisions between "welfare" recipients and non-welfare social policy recipients. And they should aim in the medium term to weaken existing strict divisions between work and non-work.

Most of these criteria can be translated into workable indices - the problem is much less one of measurement than of building a political consensus for such an effort. The question is whether such criteria would last long without becoming empty expressions. Why would even well-intentioned, public-spirited groups not quickly return to interest-group competition? What would block bureaucratic proliferation and institutional fragmentation? Would not a dynamic reappear similar to that which rendered social policies vulnerable to the conservative critique?

There is no guarantee that new welfare initiatives would not fail because of this dynamic. But there are two reasons to think a different outcome is possible. First, the actors may have reason to act as though narrow interest-group behaviour would be counterproductive, given their prior experiences. Second, the pressure of the conservative critique may force a kind of discipline on those in favour of more active social policies. If so, this would be because electoral success depends upon presenting programmes which conform to the criteria outlined above, and arguing persuasively for a broader vision than one of returning to what conservatives have called the "social pork barrel".

Ongoing socio-economic changes allow shifting the argument about economic and social rationality in a new direction. New social policy initatives can play an important developmental role in coming decades, helping to shape the outcome of turbulent processes of transition. This possibility allows a new response to the conservative critique of the welfare state: growth cannot be presumed, but sustained socio-economic development requires an expansion and renewal of social policy efforts. If this argument can be made effectively in politics, then a durable connection can be made between modernising and democratic claims.

References

Bawden, D. Lee, and John L. Palmer, 1984.
"Social Policy: Challenging the Welfare State". In *The Reagan Record*, edited by John L. Palmer and Isabel V. Sawhill. Cambridge: Ballinger.

Bell, Daniel, and Irving Kristol, editors, 1981.
The Crisis in Economic Theory. New York: Basic Books.

Block, Fred, 1984.
"Technological Displacement and Long-Term Work Trends". Unpublished manuscript.

Berger, Peter L., and Richard Neuhaus, 1977.
To Empower People: The Role of Mediating Structures in Public Policy. Washington: American Enterprise Institute.

Bowles, Samuel, David M. Gordon, and Thomas E. Weisskopf, 1983.
Beyond the Waste Land: A Democratic Alternative to Economic Decline. Garden City, New York: Doubleday.

Burnham, Walter Dean, 1982.
The Current Crisis in American Politics. New York: Oxford University Press.

Crawford, Alan, 1980.
Thunder on the Right: The "New Right" and the Politics of Resentment. New York: Pantheon.

Ehrenreich, Barbara, and Frances Fox Piven, 1984.
"Women and the Welfare State". In *Alternatives: Proposals for American from the Democratic Left*, edited by Irving Howe. New York: Pantheon.

Friedman, Milton, 1983.
Bright Promises, Dismal Performance: An Economist's Protest. New York: Harcourt Brace Jovanovich.

Gartner, Alan, Colin Greer, and Frank Riessman, editors, 1984.
Beyond Reagan: Alternatives for the 80s. New York: Harper and Row.

Gilder, George, 1981.
Wealth and Poverty. New York: Basic Books.

Glazer, Nathan, 1976.
Affirmative Discrimination: Ethnic Inequality and Public Policy. New York: Basic Books.

—,1984.
"The Social Policy of the Reagan Administration: A Review" *The Public Interest* Number 75, Spring 1984: 76-98.

Huntington, Samuel P., 1981.
American Politics - The Promise of Disharmony.
Cambridge: Harvard University Press.
Kristol, Irving, 1978.
Two Cheers for Capitalism. New York: Basic Books.
Moon, Marilyn, and Isabel V. Sawhill, 1984.
"Family Incomes: Gainers and Losers". In *The Reagan Record*, edited by John L. Palmer and Isabel V. Sawhill.
Cambridge: Ballinger.
Moynihan, Daniel, 1969.
Maximum Feasible Misunderstanding. New York: Free Press.
Nathan, Richard P., 1983.
"The Reagan Presidency in Domestic Affairs". In *The Reagan Presidency: An Early Assessment*, edited by Fred I. Greenstein. Baltimore: Johns Hopkins University Press.
Offe, Claus, 1984.
Contradictions of the Welfare State. Cambridge: MIT Press.
Pertschuk, Michael, 1982.
Revolt Against Regulation. Berkeley: University of California Press.
Phillips, Kevin, 1983.
Post-Conservative America: People, Politics, and Ideology in a Time of Crisis. New York: Vintage.
Piven, Frances Fox, and Richard A. Cloward, 1971.
Regulating the Poor: The Functions of Public Welfare. New York: Random House.
— , 1982.
The New Class War: Reagan's Attack on the Welfare State and its Consequences. New York: Pantheon.
Reich, Robert, 1983.
The Next American Frontier. New York: Penguin.
Salisbury, Robert, H., 1979.
"Why No Corporatism in America?". In *Trends Toward Corporatist Intermediation*, edited by Philippe C. Schmitter and Gerhard Lehmbruch. Beverley Hills: Sage.
Sears, David O., and Jack Citrin, 1982.
Tax Revolt: Something for Nothing in California.
Cambridge: Harvard University Press.
Sowell, Thomas, 1980.
Knowledge and Decisions. New York: Basic Books.
Steinfels, Peter, 1979.
The Neoconservatives. New York: Simon and Schuster.
Therborn, Goran, 1984.
"The Prospects of Labour and the Transformation of Advanced Capitalism". *New Left Review* Number 145, May-June: 5-38.

Whitaker, Robert W., editor, 1982.
  The New Right Papers. New York: St. Martin's Press.
Will, George F., 1983.
  Statecraft as Soulcraft. New York: Simon and Schuster.

ON THE COMPATIBILITY OF THE
WELFARE STATE
AND THE MARKET ECONOMY

J.A.H. Maks*

Abstract

Very broadly one may divide the economists nowadays into two or three parties. One party believes in the market economy: Austrians and monetarists with theories of the market economy that insufficiently satisfy their opponents. This party opposes government intervention on both the macro and the micro level. On the other hand one has the believers in government intervention and regulation. On the macro level: the Keynesians to be subdivided in Hydraulicists, educated in the mainstream textbook macro-economics, Post-Keynesians, who emphasise expectations, uncertainty and animal spirits, and the Reductionists, those who try to find a choice-theoretical basis for macro-economics. The welfare economists guide government intervention on the micro level. Unfortunately, this branch of economics is not very authoritative among the profession nor the politicians. However, it is perfectly clear that the welfare state urgently needs a theory that can serve as a guideline for its interventions on the micro level.

In this paper it is attempted to remedy various deficiencies of welfare economies by applying some results of modern partial market theory to a general systems theory. This amounts to be an analysis of a sequence of temporary barrier market equilibria. The implications are that slow rates of entry in markets and high concentration rates do not necessarily prevent competition leading to growth and technical progress; temporary, perishable barriers of entry stimulate both; by diminishing entrepreneurial incentives and responsibilities the welfare state hampers the occurence of such competition; by consequence the creation of demand for new types of labour is frustrated, whereas the demand for old types of labour decreases or vanishes and structural unemployment develops to high natural rates; the tax and social security system associated with the welfare state in its present form reduces the propensity to build up new types of human capital or to supply labour at markets on which one does not need to offer by virtue of the regulations.

---

* I would like to thank L. Hoogduin, S.K. Kuipers, J. Muysken and J. Snippe for valuable comments.

Since the theory is able to diagnose the impact of the welfare state in its present form on the market economy as modelled in a sequence of temporary barrier market equilibria, we can also suggest some policy improvements such that the basic goals of the welfare state (full employment and a fair social security system) may become compatible with a growing, technically progressive market economy producing competitive and high quality consumer and producer goods. In this sense the theory may clarify the compatibility of the welfare state and the market economy.

1. Introduction

A welfare state is a form of intervention or "dirigiste" state. An essential characteristic of the latter is the regularity of state intervention in situations in which parties are opposed in such a way that intervention is *assumed* to be useful. In the Netherlands the rise of the interventionist state was initiated by the classical liberals /1/ around the beginning of this century with the Pierson-Goeman Borgesius government (1897-1901) / 2/. Its extension evolved in three phases. The first period, characterised by tendencies towards corporatism, lasted from 1930 until 1950. In the second one, from 1950 until 1965, a social security system was established and in the last period from 1965 until, say, 1975, the emphasis was on 'well-being': the attention focused on environmental problems, dispersion of knowledge, a more equal income distribution and more democracy in the workplace. The interventionist state of these last two periods may well be conceived as the Dutch realisation of the welfare state.

Formulated in economic terms, the interventionist state can be considered as revealing the fact that 'one' does not rely on the results from freely negotiated agreements in the market process. Since the welfare state intervenes in this process on the macro and the micro level an economic theory to guide or to evaluate these policies may be helpful. If the state of the economic art is reviewed very broadly one gets the following picture.

On the one hand one has the Keynesians. They can be subdivided in Hydraulicists /3/, educated in the mainstream textbook macro-economics, Post-Keynesians with their em-

---

1. 'Classical' is added here to avoid confusion with the contemporary meaning attached to 'liberal' in the Anglo Saxon area.
2. See J.W. de Beus (8), especially p. 103-104.
3. This subdivision has been derived from Coddington (9).

phasis on expectations, uncertainty and animal spirits, and Reductionists /3/, who try to find a choice theoretical basis for macro-economics. The main policy recommendation of the Hydraulicists entails the manipulation of the 'effective demand' with fiscal and monetary instruments to control the business cycle and to maintain full employment. The Post-Keynesians reject the until the 70s fairly well accepted, neoclassical synthesis /4/ of the Hydraulicists. They see a prices and incomes policy to diminish inflation as a necessary adjunct to the above mentioned traditional instruments, together with some social mechanism (e.g. indicative planning together with selective public sector planning) to direct the amount and type of investment so as to increase the growth rate of the national product /5/. The Reductionists acknowledge the possibility of the existence of different regimes. Each regime implies a characteristic and different set of policy implications. The main analytical feature is the use of a choice theoretical framework frequently at the aggregate level with, additionally, quantity contraints /6/. Thus far the policy implications are not clearly and generally established, but an influential author does not hesitate to consider the real wage rate as a policy instrument /7/.

On the other hand one has the Monetarists and the Neo-Austrians. They believe in an adequate functioning of the market economy. The Monetarists recommend much less government intervention than we have nowadays in most Western developed economies combined with a simple growth rule of money supply. The Neo-Austrian insight also strongly opposes government intervention, returning to the minimum state or even less than that. They even disapprove of the Monetarist controlled supply of 'state money'. Hayek, for example, sees a competitive market system to supply money as an efficient instrument to tackle inflation. Like the Monetarists, the Neo-Austrians are inclined to blame state intervention for a lot of undesired consequences. They maintain for example that in the U.S.A. the length of the Great Depression of the 30s was severely extended by government intervention /8/.

This paper is not the suitable context for a thorough evaluation of these various schools of throught from a theoretical and empirical point of view. We see a diminishing popularity of

---

4. This term is introduced by Samuelson. The synthesis is fundamentally based on Hicks' interpretation of Keynes (20), given in Hicks (18).
5. See for example A.S. Eichner (12).
6. This theoretical development starts with Patinkin (28). Important contributions are made by Barro and Grossman (5) and Malinvaud (21).
7. See Malinvaud (21).
8. See Rothbard (32).

Keynesian theories and policies in the seventies and an increase in scientific and political interest in the Monetarist theories. We observe that in Keynesian types of analysis no attention is paid to changes in relative prices and their consequences *within* the few aggregates that are usually used: one consumer good, one kind of labour, etc. The Keynesian position maintains that the proposed macro-interventions correct undesired consequences of the functioning of a free market allocation process. However, the Keynesian analyses can hardly be conceived as a suitable basis for the guidance of the micro-interventions of the welfare state.

The Monetarists and the Neo-Austrians share their objections to macro and micro-interventions. An important Monetarist contribution with a tremendous impact is the rational expectations hypothesis. An analytically related position is their confidence in the ability of the market to approach closely to a Pareto-optimal intertemporal co-ordination, without government intervention. In the next section this ability will be questioned. The Neo-Austrians do not believe in this ability either. But they see the market process as by far the most efficient way to improve the co-ordination, because in this process 'tacit' knowledge of the economic subjects is revealed and used, whereas there is no way a government will ever be able to utilise this knowledge /9/.

From these considerations we conclude that neither Keynesian nor Monetarist or Neo-Austrian insights constitute a suitable basis for guiding and evaluating the micro-interventions of the welfare state. The regular candidate to perform this task is welfare economics. This branch of economics does not share the Monetarist claim that a free market process approaches closely to intertemporal Pareto-optimal co-ordination. Nevertheless it does take this co-ordination as norm together with perfect competition. Given these ideals welfare economics attempts to advise micro-interventions with a more or less open eye for the difference between the ideal and reality /10/. However, welfare economics does not have much impact on micro-intervention policies and is not very authoritative among economists. It is the main purpose of this paper to develop in a rather unprecise, preliminary and informal way a welfare theory with more realistic ideals. The plan of the paper is as follows. In Section two it is proposed to replace the intertemporal Pareto-optimal co-ordination norm by Pareto-optimality in

---

9. See Hayek (16).
10. See F. Hartog (15).

each period supplemented by the requirement of for example, a potential Pareto-improvement in each successive period. Moreover it is suggested to replace perfect foresight-like assumptions by bounded rational expectation hypotheses. In Section three it is attempted to formulate a kind of barrier market theory. This barrier market model is used to replace the perfect competition model in a sequence of temporary equilibria with bounded rational expectations. In the final section an attempt is undertaken to derive some policy implications of the developed theory.

2. Intertemporal versus temporary equilibria

The simple context for Pareto-optimality is a static, or one period, general equilibrium model. The well known restrictions of this approach are:
1. it is not intertemporal, growth and technical progress are not analysed:
2. expectations and imperfect information do not play any role:
3. it is based on perfect competition, hence 'genuine' competition and entrepreneurial activities are missing.

A first multi-period analysis has been formally developed by Arrow and Debreu (2) and McKenzie (22). Equipped with sufficient assumptions this system can guarantee the existence of an intertemporal Pareto-optimal equilibrium. An important part of these assumptions entails the existence of a complete system of future markets for all goods of all future periods. Alternatively one may assume perfect information about all future equilibrium prices. The basic point is of course that the agents decide on the basis of *all* equilibrium prices. A second type of model is not only intertemporal, but also deals with uncertainty and expectations. Important contributors are Arrow (1), Debreu (10) and Radner (30). It is assumed that a finite number of states of the world can be distinguished. Each state defines the distribution of commodity stocks, the production possibilities and all kinds of other factors apart from prices which influence supply and demand. The consumer is assumed to attach subjective probabilities to each state. All contracts are consummated in the first period and they concern contingent claims for future delivery and purchase, *i.e.* contingent on the realisation of a given state. Hence a complete system of contingent future markets should exist. Alternatively one may assume this system to be incomplete and add *contingent* perfect price predictions. In this context this assumption may be denoted as a rational expectation hypothesis /11/. Under suitable assumptions this approach again guarantees the existence of intertemporal Pareto-optimal equilibria.

It is very obvious that for intertemporal Pareto-optimality one needs (conditional) perfect foresight or some equivalent set of assumptions about the existence of future markets. However, the uncertainty about future scarcity relations is a fundamental assumption of economic science, as Robbins posits /12/. Perfect foresight is only an approximating step towards a more realistic theory. It may be useful to consider how Walras, the founder of the general equilibrium approach, deals with this problem. We find a remarkable quotation at the end of his more formal analysis:

'Such is the continuous market, which is perpetually tending towards equilibrium without ever actually attaining it, because the market has no other way of approaching equilibrium except by groping, and, before the goal is reached, it has to renew its efforts and start over again, all the basic data of the problem, e.g. the initial quantities possessed, the utilities of goods and services, the technical coefficients, the excess of income over consumption, the working capital requirements, etc., having changed in the meantime.

'It can happen and frequently does happen in the real world, that under some circumstances a selling price will remain long periods of time above cost of production and continue to rise in spite of increases in output, while under other circumstances, a fall in price, following upon this rise, will suddenly bring the selling price below cost of production and force entrepreneurs to reverse their production policies. For, just as a lake is, at times, stirred to its very depths by a storm, so also the market is sometimes thrown into violent confusion by crises, which are sudden and general disturbances of equilibrium' /13/.

From this quotation we may, firstly, grasp the significance of Walras' equilibrium concept and, secondly, conclude that Walras' equilibrium was not based on perfect foresight. Its beginning indicates permanent changes in demand and supply in unforeseen ways. The equilibrium position is obviously determined by *imperfect* expectations, since disappointments permanently prevail. It can be considered as a reference point to which a market economy with sufficient competition develops, while the reference point itself permanently moves. The price expectations that Walras implicitly uses are extremely simple: the agents assume that the momentary equilibrium prices will

---

11. See for example Hildenbrand (19), pp. 1-31.
12. See Robbins (31), p. 93-94.
13. See Walras (38), p. 382.

also prevail in the future. In his formal analysis Walras assumes that the changes occur *between* the periods, so that each period has its own non-moving reference point, as can be demonstrated by the following quotations:

> '*Again our problem is to reach equilibrium in capital formation above in precisely the same way that we reached equilibrium earlier, first in exchange and then in production. In other words, we propose to start by assuming the arbitrary data of our problem to be constant over a certain period of time, and subsequently we shall suppose them to change in order to study the effects of such changes.*
> '*Thus equilibrium in capital formation will first be established in principle. Then it will be established effectively by the reciprocal exchange between saving to be accumulated and new capital goods to be supplied within a given period of time, during which no change in the data is allowed. Although the economy is becoming progressive, it remains (for the time being) static because of the fact that the new capital goods play no part in the economy until later in a period subsequent to the one under consideration*' /14/.

This type of analysis is now known as the method of temporary equilibrium and is often ascribed to Hicks /15/. But with Morishima and Diewert /16/ one may agree that Walras was basically concerned with a temporary equilibrium.

Of course, if we add *rational* expectations to a model analysing a sequence of temporary equilibria one may obtain intertemporal Pareto-optimal co-ordination. However, in the approach proposed in this paper we reject, with Walras and Robbins, the rational expectations hypothesis *and* intertemporal Pareto-optimality as a feasible co-ordination norm. Nevertheless, it remains possible to attain a Pareto-optimal allocation within a given period given the agents' non-rational expectations. Because this latter term might be confusing we will use the expression "bounded rationality" in the rest of this paper to denote all kinds of non-rational expectation formation processes, such as adaptive, unit-elastic and optimal cost expectations. In the third section we will specify the kind of expectation formation in the proposed theory of a sequence of temporary barrier market equilibria. If we accept Pareto-optimality within a period as the co-ordination norm for each period we only need to 'make the best of it' in the sense that no pair of agents will voluntarily exchange to improve the allocative co-ordination in the period

---

14. See Walras (38), p. 282.
15. See Hicks (17).
16. See Morishima (25), pp. 78-79. For a review of the developments within this approach see Drazen (11).

under consideration given the prevailing expectations. This norm may be supplemented by accepting potential Pareto-improvements as desirable for each subsequent period, for an improvement within a period and for an ordering of two series of equilibria and with requirements regarding the extent of intertemporal unco-ordination of labour markets. This point shall be elaborated in Section 4.2.

3. The barrier market in a sequence of temporary equilibria

In this section the barrier market theory is developed that is going to replace the perfect competition model in the sequence of temporary equilibria. In subsection 3.1 the essentials of the contestable market of Baumol et al., are sketched /17/. It turns out that this theory can be compatible with Pareto-optimality without leaning on the property of a great number of competitors as perfect competition does. But in subsection 3.2. it is argued that this theory, considered in a sequence of temporary equilibria, has certain shortcomings. It neglects the resurrection of barriers to entry as an important aspect in the competitive process. In subsection 3.3 a barrier market theory is presented that does not neglect this aspect, but remains at the same time compatible with Pareto-optimality. Finally the development of a sequence of temporary barrier market equilibria is analysed in subsection 3.4.

3.1 The contestable market in a static context

The most essential property of the contestable market theory is that, whatever the type of market in the traditional sense, the equilibrium price normally equals the minimum average costs and, hence, the marginal costs, if a market is contestable. This implies, if we have such contestable market equilibria everywhere in the economy, that a good stage is set to obtain Pareto-optimality. The explanation of these properties proceeds as follows. A market is contestable if it has free entry. Entry is free, apart from legal restrictions, if exit is costless. A costless exit implies that a producer is able to cover the costs emanating from his entry to the market, if he leaves the market. If a market is contestable in this sense every incumbent is vulnerable to underbidding as soon as he sets his price higher than the minimum average cost (including a normal profit). In such a case a potential entrant may hit, take his above normal profit and, if necessary, run away. If there is a threat of potential entry it is assumed that the incumbents charge the minimum average costs.

---

17. See Baumol (6) and Baumol et al., (7).

To obtain these results one does not need a great number of competitors, one incumbent and one attentive potential entrant may be sufficient, under the proviso that the extent of the market demand co-operates. This can be clarified in Figure 1. We see that the average-cost curve (AC) is assumed to re-

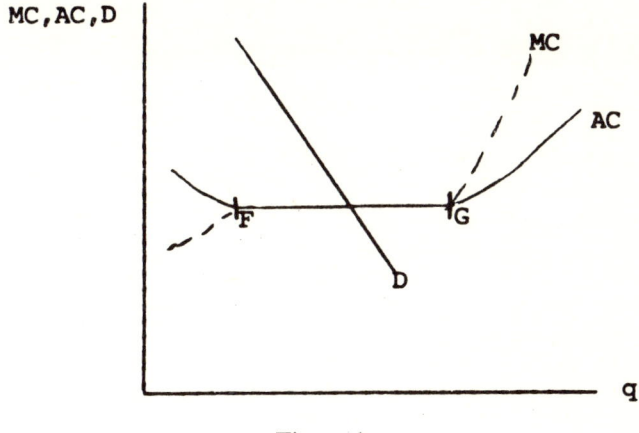

Figure 1

main constant over a substantial interval (FG) at the level of the minimum average cost. According to Baumol this assumption in not too far from reality /18/. If the extent of the market demand D is such as to intersect the average cost curve in the interval FG, the price equals minimum average cost. This horizontality assumption is especially very useful if the establishment of a market equilibrium needs a *small* number of incumbents.

From these considerations one may conclude that the contestable market looks like an attractive replacement of the old ideal of perfect competition. The contestable market equilibrium may occur with a small number of incumbents. Potential competition plays a role, products are usually offered at prices equal to marginal and minimum average cost and the general market equilibrium may easily be Pareto-optimal in this static context. Although this type of market theory still produces an ideal that is not very close to reality, it seems much closer to reality than perfect competition.

18. See Baumol (6), p. 9. Indeed, most empirical cost studies indicate that this assumption is a tenable one. See F.M. Scherer (34) especially p. 96-97 and Shepard (35), p. 245-250.

3.2. Some deficiencies of the contestable market in a sequence of temporary equilibria

In a sequence of temporary contestable market equilibria the consumers, as demanders of final products, seem to be highly served: goods can be bought as cheap as possible in every period. To remain in the market it is vital for the producer to apply the cheapest production techniques, techniques in which the technical knowlegde is optimally applied. Yet, there is a snake in the grass. Each innovation is immediately common knowledge, because the market in every, hence also in the next, period is assumed to be contestable. It seems the natural inclination of the profit seeking entrepreneur however, to raise barriers that hinder potential entrants by creating a cost advantage of some continuity. In a series of temporary contestable market equilibria innovation is necessarily a collective good. Olson (17) made it plausible that trying to acquire a collective good is generally not a rational kind of action for an individual agent. This point is also applicable here and this seems to be devastating for the implementation of the progress of science in contestable markets. It appears that Schumpeter's judgement that perfect competition is not an ideal environment for growth and technical progress is also applicable to the contestable market.

We may even generalise this critique in the following way. As stated in the preceding section costless exit is an essential property of the contestable market. If it is not costless, there are sunk costs. Current examples are: a sales distribution network, product differentiation, special expertise of hired labour, exclusive rights on production factors and, as just dealt with, exclusive knowledge of production techniques. All these examples are barriers to entry in the sense that exit is not costless anymore. They can also be seen as, possibly non-physical, capital goods rendering their services to the production process. Even if the potential entrant would be able to buy these barriers, he could not run freely because of the sunk costs. The contestable market theory cannot cope with these phenomena. Hence it necessarily neglects important aspects of the competitive process.

3.3 The barrier market, minimum average costs and Pareto-optimality

In this subsection a barrier market theory is developed that generates prices equal to the minimum average cost of the incumbents.

Important contributions in the entry barrier theory are made by Bain (4), Stigler (37), Ferguson (13) and Von Weiszäcker (41). The common conclusion of their various theories is that an entry barrier leads to higher than minimum average cost prices. Apart from the fact that empirical research does not provide much support for this thesis /19/, one can also make an analytical point in favour of a price setting behaviour close to minimum average costs in this context.

A first simplified analysis considers an equi-barrier market in a multi-period setting. This concept admits sunk costs but at the same time assumes equal exit costs for both incumbents and potential entrants. This situation prevents the hit and run activities of the contestable market. However, if one assumes that the potential entrant perceives the observed prices as reliable indicators of the minimum average cost of the incumbents, it is still very dangerous to set prices higher than these costs. The potential entrant has no reason to hesitate about entry if he thinks that the expelled competitor is unlikely to react because of his higher costs. So, again, the price setting behaviour may remain close to the minimum cost under the threat of potential entry /20/.

The more general case of the barrier market acknowledges the possibility of higher exit costs for potential entrants. Nevertheless price setting behaviour in the neighbourhood of the minimal average cost may be generated if the incumbents are aware of alert potential entrants, say existing capable enterprises who are able to quickly convert a barrier market with above normal profit opportunities to their advantage. This awareness induces cautious price setting behaviour because a higher price may stimulate entry within a short number of periods. It may also strengthen the attempts to create new barriers, leading to cheaper and better products. Such attempts are compatible with a series of barrier market equilibria, but not with a contestable market sequence. In this context the approach of Von Weiszäcker should be mentioned. His analysis focuses on social optimal barriers, but remains rather vague in specifying this concept.

---

19. See Scherer (34), especially p. 229-266.

20. The same conclusion can be obtained if we assume a trade-off by the incumbents between an above normal profit and the higher chance of expulsion. This principle can be modelled as follows. If we denote the incumbent's chance of remaining in the market with $P(R)$ and his chance of expulsion with $1 - P(R)$ then a plausible distribution function for $P(R)$ is $P(R) = 1 - c$, where $O \leqslant c \leqslant 1$ and c is equal to p, the above normal profit, related to the exit costs u. From this assumption it follows that the chance of expulsion equals zero if the above normal profit is zero. The expected value of the above normal profit minus exit costs is maximal if

$$E(p - u) = \max_{c} \left\{ P(R).c.u - (1 - p(R)).u \right\}$$

The latter expression has a maximum for $c = 0$. Hence the optimal choice implies price-setting on the level of the minimum average costs.

The supplementary norms proposed above can be used to specify 'optimality' requirements of barrier creation, if for example, one accepts the norm of a sequence of potential Pareto-superior equilibria. The creation of barriers under the effective threat of attentive potential entrants will probably lead to lower costs and higher quality for the consumers.

Thus far it is assumed that an entry will lead to the complete expulsion of the incumbent. This is, of course, a stylised fact that can be relaxed. The *enlargement* of a market share by an incumbent as a consequence of his successful attempts to create new barriers can analytically be considered as the act of a new entrant, whereas the lost market share can be seen as the disappearance of an incumbent. From these and the preceding observations one can conclude that this barrier market theory produces a perspective in which prices tend to equal minimum average costs, and in which competition leads to lower costs and to better products.

3.4. A sequence of barrier market equilibria

A thorough analysis of a sequence of temporary barrier market equilibria needs a formal analysis /21/. Thus the following argumentation is rather preliminary. However it is hoped that the contours of the development of such a sequence, although necessarily vague, can be sufficiently substantial and general.

The equilibrium concept nowadays also includes equilibria with quantity rationing. For various reasons we will restrict our analysis to Arrow-Debreu temporary equilibria, i.e. we assume that the incumbents are sufficiently aware of alert potential entrants; we assume a sufficient number of potential entrants, and a co-operative extent of the market demands. However, this assumption can be hindered by exogeneous factors causing rationing or fixed prices. As an example one may think of a market to which entry with kinds of competitive activities is blocked by government intervention. The temporary equilibrium approach immediately raises the question in what sense there can be involuntary unemployment. As already stated the proposed theory will be based on bounded rational expectations. This implies that intertemporal unco-ordinated situations can prevail or, equivalently, intertemporal disequilibria in the goods and labour markets. However, since the analysis assumes temporary equilibria without rationing, the expectations of the period under consideration are not disappointed. On the other hand one may have non-essential equilibria on a number of labour

---

21. This analysis will be started in the context of a research project 'The barrier market in a sequence of temporary equilibria' of the Department of Economics of the University of Groningen.

markets, i.e. there is no exchange of those labour services in the period under consideration. These cases may indicate the genesis of a new type of labour demand, whereas supply has yet to come or the supply of a traditional skill with no demand in the present period. So one might consider measuring the extent of intertemporal unco-ordinated situations in a given period on the basis of the number of non-essential equilibria. It is to be added in this context that this idea of measuring the extent of intertemporally disappointed expectations through the number of non-exchange equilibria should only be applied to labour services that are in exchange in a specified part of the sequence of temporary equilibria.

The development on the numerous labour markets with respect to the mitigation of such intertemporal "unemployment" and on the numerous good markets with regard to decreasing costs and improving quality depends basically in this analysis on:
(1) the extent to which producers and consumers are able to predict the changes in the demand of the final goods and services and of the labour and other productive goods and services;
(2) the rate with which barriers to entry are constructed, their quality and the effectiveness of the competitive threat of the potential entrants.

The first point implies that to the extent that the expectations are more rational, dovetailing of supply and demand with *exchange* will occur more often. It is to be noted however that, because we did accept bounded rationality, it will never be a perfect match. One may even have, because of sudden new technological possibilities for instance, sequences with substantial numbers of mismatches. On this point it is useful to insert an expectation formation hypothesis. It will be assumed that the agents try and succeed in their relevant markets to acquire more rational expectations, the more the expected advantages or disadvantages of the venture are a reward or loss for the decision maker himself. Profit and income perspectives are assumed to be helpful incentives in the dovetailing process of (1). The second point is also determined by the perceived income and profit at stake. These are clearly the motives to erect the barriers to entry for producers, but also for the consumers as owners of human capital, the services of which they try to sell on the various labour markets. But also the attentiveness of potential entrants is obviously determined by these incentives. The weakening of the attention of an incumbent can be expected to be corrected by an attentive potential entrant, but only if the incentives are worthwhile. This point rests on the principle of the trade-off between the expected gains and the effects and sacrifices to get them.

So far we formulated as co-ordination norm for our analysis Pareto-optimality in each period supplemented with potential Pareto superiority of the successive temporary equilibria. This supplement may be extended to imply some requirements on the number of labour markets in non-exchange equilibria, say some minimum over a number of periods, given the 'best' bounded rational expectations.

In this way it is hoped that the stage is sufficiently set to derive some policy implications in the next section. In the meantime it may be worthwhile to direct the attention to Walras' description of the competitive process in barrier market conditions /22/.

'More often, the commodity, while remaining essentially the same, is given a slightly different form to sell at different prices. For example, a manufacturer who sells chocolate wrapped in plain glazed paper and modestly labelled 'Superfine' at 3 francs a pound, will charge 4 francs a pound for the same chocolate with a little vanilla flavour added, wrapped in gilt paper and advertised as 'Royal'. It is readily seen, however, that, under a regime of free competition, it is much more difficult to continue playing these artful tricks, precisely because the differences in price, which are appreciably greater than the costs of producing discriminative forms and labels, tend constantly to be narrowed by competition. A competitor will soon enter the field of our chocolate manufacturer and sell 'Royal' chocolate at 3 francs 80 centimes a pound, which will compel our original manufacturer to offer it at 3 francs 60 centimes, so that the competitor, in turn, will bring his price down to 3 francs 40 centimes and force the original manufacturer to lower his price to 3 francs 30 centimes.'

4. The policy implications

The preliminary character of the analysis of a sequence of temporary barrier market equilibria has been emphasised in the preceding section. Nevertheless, the general nature of the policy implications appears to be rather manifest.

This section contains a first, incomplete and rather superficial attempt to describe these implications. In subsection 4.1 it is discussed whether government intervention in the developed theory of a sequence of temporary barrier market equilibria will be able to realise intertemporal Pareto-optimal allocation. The next subsection reconsiders temporary Pareto-optimality

---

22. See Walras (38), pp. 442-443.

as the norm and evaluates Ng's contribution with regard to first best rules. In subsection 4.3 some first best policy proposals are proposed, whereas in subsection 4.4 a number of policy proposals with regard to the supplementary norms are analysed. The final subsection deals with the question of what will happen in a barrier market economy if typical welfare state intervention occurs.

4.1. Government intervention and intertemporally Pareto-optimal co-ordination

The developed theory diminishes the well known second best problem in the sense that the proposed barrier market model may be considered, or at least has the pretention to be more realistic than the perfect competition model. On the other hand we observe that the temporary equilibria, because of the bounded rational expectation hypothesis, will not be intertemporally Pareto-optimal co-ordinated. Thus one may wonder whether government interventions may be able to realise this co-ordination in a second best approach. Mishan (14) mitigates the second-best problem by positing that it is less relevant for the exchange and the production optimum than for the optimum in which the subjective and technical ratios should be dovetailed. However, if we take imperfect foresight as a necessary starting point it is clear that even the exchange and production optimum will be hampered by the lack of intertemporal co-ordination. From the literature devoted to the second best problem in a purely static context, it turns out very obviously that the obtained rules lead to informational requirements far beyond what is possible to produce in practice /23/. This situation is most seriously worsened if considered in a multi-period context with intertemporal Pareto-optimality as co-ordination norm. To this observation one may add that it is questionable whether a government *in principle* is able to acquire information of a quality that can compete with the quality of the expectations of the private agents /24/. This follows from the assumption that expectations will be more rational, up to a point, the more the decision maker himself benefits or loses as a consequence of the action he choses to undertake. However, the government as decision-maker, almost by definition, does not serve it's own interest /25/. Moreover the private agents, in informing the government, may manipulate their messages in

---

23. See for example Sandler (33), Starret (36), Guesnerie (14), Walsh (39), Ng (26).
24. See page 116.
25. If it does, and there are theories elaborating the assumption, the conclusions point strongly in the direction of a minimum state.

their own interest. From these considerations we conclude that government intervention will *not* be able to realise intertemporally perfect co-ordination.

4.2. Temporary Pareto-optimality and Ng's policy proposals

As stated above, our approach proposes to use as co-ordination norm:

(1) Pareto-optimality in each successive period supplemented with;
(2) requirements of potential Pareto superiority of the successive equilibria and of a minimum number of non-exchange equilibria in the labour markets in such a series.

In this and the next subsection the first norm will be considered and the second norm will be dealt with in subsection 4.4.

It is very obvious that a Pareto-optimal equilibrium in a period is determined by the prevailing bounded rational expectations. In such a setting one might question the sense of choosing temporary Pareto-optimality as norm. To this point one can make the following remarks:

– the question can be raised to each voluntary transaction: it is advantageous for the parties involved given their expectations;
– in the temporary Pareto-optimal barrier market equilibrium products are traded as cheaply as possible and in the best possible quality;
– any argument leading to a preference for another allocation in a period must be based on its Pareto-superiority with reference to future prices. It then just indicates *different* expectations: the preferred allocation may be the temporary Pareto-optimum given these different expectations;
– according to the supplementary norm in our modified welfare theory the number of intertemporal unco-ordinations on the labour markets is assumed to be 'minimised' by virtue of the expectation formation hypothesis /26/.

If these points are sufficiently convincing, one may consider striving after Pareto-optimality, or less ambitious, potential Pareto-improvements with the following policy proposals of Ng /27/.

Yew-Kwang Ng distinguishes the quality of information in three classes:

(1) informational poverty: the quality of the information is insufficient to establish a reasonable probability estimate *with regard to (a)* the direction and the extent to which the second best optimum deviates from the situation that

---

26. See page 116.
27. See Ng (26), especially p. 224.

would result with application of first best rules, if no second best constraints exist, and *with regard to (b)* the position and skewness fo the relation curve, defined in the appendix, apart from its concavity;
(2) informational scarcity: the information is sufficient to direct a probability estimate with regard to (a) and (b);
(3) perfect information.

Because in the preceding perfect information has been rejected, the first two classes are relevant. Ng proposes 'first best' rules to apply in situation (1) and 'third best' rules in situation (2) /28/. This advice can be applied without any amendment in the case of our temporary Paret-optimum /29/.

How should one evaluate Ng's proposals. Let us firstly assess a situation with informational poverty. Here Ng suggests the use of first best rules. If, for example, this would mean: 'apply the price = marginal cost rule in the sense that a government committee should calculate marginal costs' this proposal would make less sense in our approach. For the marginal costs also depend on future prices and it is questionable that such a committee will be able to produce good quality price expectations. If, on the other hand, the rule guides a policy that stimulates potential competition by for example deleting a legalised barrier to entry, such application is quite compatible with the proposed welfare theory. Ng's proposal in situations with informational scarcity should be considered with some reluctancy. It presupposes some government knowledge of the relevant influence of current and future restrictions on the relation curve /30/. So this policy proposal always needs government price expectations.

4.3. Some first best policy proposals
In this subsection some first best policy proposals will be elaborated. Attention is focused on both the good and labour markets.

Competition policy should be modelled as follows. In the barrier market theory as developed in the preceding section the barriers are under permanent pressure and check of the potential entrants. If they are misused an attentive entrant may come in and erect his own barrier and thereby destroying the barrier of the expelled competitor. This presupposes that the barriers are perishable and beatable by competitive action. From this it follows that the government should not legalise barriers in such a way that it yields permanent and unbeatable protection. Traditionally competition policy is strongly based on concen-

---

28. See the appendix.
29. Ng's proposals are explained in the appendix.
30. See the appendix for an explanation of this concept.

tration ratios, market shares and rates of entry. In the proposed approach there is no a priori bias against low rates of entry or high concentration ratios. An impeccable price setting behaviour, continuously in the neighbourhood of the minimum avarage costs may be compatible with both phenomena. The same applies to cartels in the presence of sufficient effective potential competition. Of course it is to be added emphatically that the government should *not* legalise any cartel barrier /31/. Finally, a short note on the banking system. If the banking system is legally closed for new entry, this may have tremendous negative impact in the barrier market system. Banks are then stimulated to close the markets in which their clients operate, by refusing credits to potential entrants.

The labour markets should be approached as follows. As in the cartel case there is no a priori bias against labour unions, under the important condition that the markets remain vulnerable for competitive actions of non-union member labour suppliers. Hence, closed shops are undesirable, as are agreements between labour and employers unions on national, industry or firm level, where application to non-members is enforced by law /32/. Cartel arrangements should not oblige non-members and the same principle applies here.

A final point should be raised. It has been concluded that a government should not legalise barriers in such a way that they become imperishable. It remains to be considered to what extent barriers should deserve government protection. In this context one may analyse patent rights, mark rights, copyrights, etc. In principle one would choose for a patent right leading to some 'optimal rate' of product and process innovation. This may imply some degree of protection to make the innovation sufficiently worthwile, but not too long and too general. Potential competition should not loose the strength of its threat in the eyes of the incumbent. This point however deserves further elaboration.

4.4. The supplementary norms and their policy instruments

In this subsection we will be concerned with the social security and the tax system.

The social security system

Two properties of the developed barrier market theory seem to be highly relevant in this context. Firstly, the hypothesis of bounded rational expectations and secondly the assumption that the quality of the agents' price expectations can be posi-

---

31. In Dutch terms: algemeen verbindend verklaren.
32. See note 31.

tively influenced the more they are held responsible for the consequences of their decisions. The first hypothesis implies clearly that there will be unforeseeable, involuntary, intertemporal unco-ordinations in the market process. Agents will lose their jobs or will go bankrupt. This leads to the desirability of implementing this net as a social, i.e., largely controlled by government regulations security system, then the second assumption offers some indications. The system should attempt to restrict its damage to the quality of the price expectations. The higher it's payments the less the agents care for the consequences of their decisions. This means for instance that the agents are less alert in the choice of the construction of the various kinds of human capital, with regard to the future prices of their services. Another factor that should be mentioned is the influence of the social security payment on the minimum income required to generate the willingness to supply a service. A higher payment increases this income. This means that the supply curve moves to the right and this will lead to less transactions in this labour market. Thus, if the network has to be social, it should preferably guarantee only some minimum income.

All insurance beyond this minimum is to be obtained in free individual agreements with private insurance companies. An advantage of this type of insurance is that the height of the premium indicates the risk involved, because it is the interest of the insurance company to estimate it as rational as possible. In such a case the government should not regulate uniform prices. The latter would prevent that the insured clients receive information regarding the extent of the risk of the business to which they sell their services.

The tax system

The traditional welfare theory prefers taxes on surplus incomes (e.g. above normal profits) and lump sum taxes on normal incomes. These kinds of taxes do not influence the marginal decisions. In our intertemporal approach this property does not hold. Above normal profits signal temporal and probably intertemporal unco-ordinated situations to the incumbents and potential entrants of a market. A tax on these surplus incomes delays the adaptation process and increases the number and length of the disequilibrium situations. Lump sum taxes on labour income should differentiate their tariffs to the different kinds of human capital and the current and expected prices of their services. If this leads to a high lump sum if the government expects high future prices, this expectation may influence the expectations of the agents. As a consequence the supply of this service will be larger than originally planned on the basis of the uninfluenced better quality expectations. We will probably end up with lower prices, not justifying the high lump sum tariff.

These considerations indicate that neutral taxes do not exist in our revised welfare theory. If this is the case we have to compromise. If we take as principle that a tax system should try to restrict its damage with regard to its negative influence on price expectations, on the construction of barriers to entry, on the alertness of the potential entrants and on the construction of new kinds of human capital, a suitable suggestion to these ends is probably a flat, moderate and *stable* rate, accepted by the vast majority of the agents.

4.5 Consequences of welfare state intervention in a barrier market economy?

We have argued that profit and income incentives are important for an adequate functioning of a barrier market economy. What then would be the influence in such an economy of high and progressive income taxes, high profit taxes, high social security premiums, partly based on income prices, of an extensive social security system, to a substantial degree transferring amounts of income unrelated to the premium paid, of income prices and of a massive subsidy system? All these measures decrease the advantages of successful operations. This observation leads to a diminished effort in trying to create successful barriers, in the attentiveness of potential entrants and in the care in the acquirement of the various kinds of human capital.

The consequences are a lower level of competitiveness, a lower growth rate of production given its level and more unemployment. These tendencies can be expected to be reinforced by the diminished degree of rationality of the expectations. On the other hand, if the disadvantages of unsuccessful operations are known to be compensated, one is less critical towards dubious undertakings. Moreover, we see in the welfare state legalised protection of barriers of entry on a very substantial scale. This observation applies to both the goods and labour markets. Without further elaboration of these points in the present context the relative weakness of the welfare state economies is illustrated in Table 1. This table gives in column 1 and 2 the welfare state index values for a number welfare state oriented Western European countries (Sweden, the Netherlands, France, West Germany, the United Kingdom) in 1960 and 1978. These countries, taken together, had a U.S. equal total employment figure in 1960. The welfare state index adds the shares (%) of direct and indirect taxes and of the share of social security contribution in the gross domestic product. Although this index is certainly not the ideal index to measure the extent of the government interventions in the market process, it may give a rough and first impression of the rate of these interventions. The same index is also calculated for the U.S.A., Switzerland and Japan, being more market-oriented economies. The increase in this index value is given in column 3. The % increase in the total labour force (ΔLF) in the period 1960-1980 is given in column 5. The % increase in total employment (ΔET) is given in column 6. The % change in employment in the market sector (ΔEMS) is estimated in column 7. Since these figures are obtained (with the exception of the Netherlands) by subtracting from the increase in total employment the increase in the share of government employees in total employment, their values should probably be lower, for they should also be corrected with the increase in employment in the semi-collective sector. Unfortunately reliable figures to add this correction were only available for the Netherlands. Nevertheless it can be clearly seen that the employment in the market sector of the Western European welfare state oriented economies is clearly shrinking, whereas the more flexible economies of the U.S.A. and Japan are able to create substantial amounts of employment in the market sector, close to the increase in their labour force, an increase that is substantially higher than in the welfare states. These states, taken together, were not able to increase their employment *at all* in the period under consideration. Finally, we see in column 7 the estimated size of their hidden economies. It is obvious again that the welfare states perform worse in this respect.

Although these questions deserve a more thorough analysis than has been given in this paper, one may observe the following: if this analysis roughly reveals the same properties and tendencies, policy decisions should be based on the dilemma: more/less of the welfare state in its present form will probably weaken/improve the functioning of the market economy.

Table 1:   The Impact of the Welfare State on Employment in the Market Sector

	1 W.S.I. 1960	2 W.S.I. 1978	3 ΔW.S.I. 1962-79	4 ΔLF 1962-79		5 ΔET 1962-79	6 ΔEMS 1978	7 ΔSBE
Sweden	28,6	53	24,4	15	(15)	14,3	−10,0	13,2
Netherlands	30,2	57	26,8	13,4	(14,5)	9,5	−10,0[b]	9,6
France	33,4	38,5	5,1	16,2	(18)	10,6	8,6[a]	9,4
FR Germany	33,9	39,9	6,7	− 1,5	(−2)	− 4,0	− 9,9	8,6
United Kingdom	27,5	34,7	5,1	5,7	(6,3)	2,0	− 5,5	8,0
U.S.A.	27,5	31,1	3,6	43,0	(46)	42,4	39,4	8,3
Switzerland	20,4	31,1	10,7	6,3	(6,3)	6,0	2,0[a]	4,3
Japan	19,3	22,2	3,0	21,3	(21,3)	20,3	17,0	4,1

Source columns 1, 2 and 3: OECD, National Accounts Statistics Various Years

Source column 4: OECD, Labour Force Statistics 1964-1975 and 1968-1979. In brackets Δcivilian labour force is (Δtotal labour force) minus (Δarmed forces).

Source column 5: OECD, Labour Force Statistics 1964-1975 and 1968-1979.

Source column 6: OECD, Labour Force Statistics 1964-1975 and 1978-1979. Also OECD, National Accounts 1962-1979. Results derived by substracting from total employment the employment in sector B i.e. producers of governement services.

Source column 7: B.S. Frey and H. Weck-Hanneman, 1984, The hidden economy as an 'unobserved' variable, *European Economic Review*, 26, 33-53.

a   Source: OECD, Labour Force Statistics 1964-1975, 1968-1979 and also Frey and Weck-Hanneman (1984), p. 49.

b   This figure is obtained by extrapolating the decrease in employ ment in the market sector over the period 1970-1980 back to 1960.
Source: Jaarverslag 1981, De Nederlandsche Bank, p. 38. This figure includes the growth of the Dutch semi-collective sector, although it still does not includes subsidised sectors such as public transport.

Appendix

Ng's policy proposals

Assume that a Paretian social welfare function L is to be maximised. Let us denote the first order partial derivative of L to its ith variable, the good under consideration, as L_i. The relation function can be defined as a function that gives the value of L as a function of L_i. In Figure 2 this relation is described by the curve L^1 in the case of the absence of second best restrictions and L^{2L} or L^{2R} in the case of the presence of these restrictions.

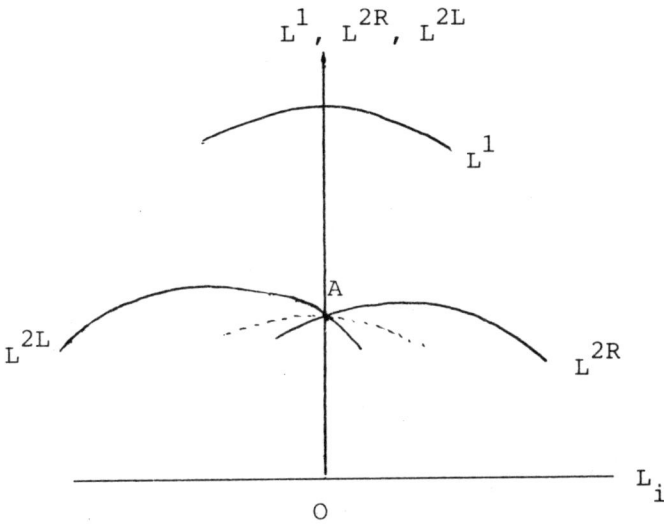

Figure 2

In the former case one has $L = 0$ if L^1 has a maximum value. In the latter case one has $L_i \neq 0$, if the objective function has a maximum. Because in the situation (1) of informational poverty we know nothing about the direction and the extent of the deviation of the relation curve of second best restrictions exist, Ng posits that a deviation to the left (L^{2L}) has the same probability as a deviation to the right (L^{2R}). Furthermore, because we do not have arguments in favour of skewness Ng assumes L^{2R} and L^{2L} not to be skew. These assumptions make it clear that the expected value of first-best rules generates a maximum. The dotted curve through A describes approximately the expected value of the objective function.

In a situation (2) of informational poverty Ng proposes third best rules. If, for example, we know something about the skewness of the relation curve but a position to the left or to the right is equally probable, one is able to derive the desired direction of the deviation of the first best position. If a deviation to one side is more probable, it may have its weight in the determination of the expected value. In this way one can estimate in which direction the expected value is higher and even where it obtains its maximum.

References

(1) Arrow, K.J., 1963-1964,
'The role of securities in the optimal allocation of risk-bearing', *Review of Economic Studies*, 31, 91-96.
(2) Arrow, K.J. and G. Debreu, 1954,
'Existence of equilibrium for a competitive economy', *Econometrica*, 22, 265-290.
(3) Arrow, K.J. and F.H. Hahn, 1971,
General Competitive Analysis, Edinburgh.
(4) Bain, J.S., 1956,
Barriers to new competition, Boston.
(5) Barro, R.J. and H.I. Grossman, 1971,
'A General Disequilibrium Model of Income and Employment', *American Economic Review*, 61, 82-93.
(6) Baumol, W.J., 1982,
'Contestable markets: an uprising in the theory of industry structure', *American Economic Review*, 72, 1-15.
(7) Baumol, W.J., J.C. Panzar and R.D. Willig, 1982,
Contestable markets and the theory of industry structure, San Diego.
(8) Beus, J.W. de, 1984,
'Oorsprong en wederkeer van de liberalen', in : J.W. de Beus and J.A.A. van Doorn (eds.), *De interventiestaat*, Meppel, 88-114.
(9) Coddington, A., 1983,
Keynesian Economics. The Search for First Principles, London.
(10) Debreu, G., 1959,
Theory of Value, New York.
(11) Drazen, A., 1980,
'Recent Developments in Macroeconomics Disquilibrium Theory', *Econometrica*, 48, 282-306.
(12) Eichner, A.S., 1977,
'A Guide to Post-Keynesian Economics'.
(13) Ferguson, J.M., 1974,
Advertising and competition: theory, measurement, fact, Cambridge (U.S.A.).
(14) Guesnerie, R., 1980,
'Second best pricing rules', *Journal of Public Economics*, 13, 51-80.
(15) Hartog, F., 1981,
Toegepaste welvaartstheorie, Leiden.
(16) Hayek, F.A., 1945,
Individualism and Economic Order, London.
(17) Hicks, J.R., 1946,
Capital and Value, Oxford.

(18) Hicks, J.R., 1937,
'Mr. Keynes and the 'Classics': a suggested interpretation',
Econometrica 5, 147-159.

(19) Hildenbrand, W., 1982,
'Information und Ressourcenallokation: Ein Uberblick' in:
Information in der Wirtschaft E. Streissler (ed.), 9-31,
Berlin.

(20) Keynes, J.M., 1936,
The General Theory of Employment, Interest and Money,
New York.

(21) Malinvaud, E., 1977,
The Theory of Unemployment Reconsidered, Oxford.

(22) McKenzie, L., 1959,
'On the existence of general equilibrium for a competitive
market', *Econometrica*, 27, 54-71.

(23) Menger, C., 1883,
*Untersuchungen uber die Methode der Sozialwissenschaften
und der politischen okonomie insbesondere*, Leipzig.

(24) Mishan, E.J., 1962,
'Second thoughts on second best', *Oxford Economic
Papers*, 14, 205-217.

(25) Morishima, M., 1977,
Walras economics, Cambridge.

(26) Ng, Y-K., 1979,
Welfare economics, London

(27) Olson, M., 1971,
The logic of collective action, Cambridge.

(28) Patinkin, D., 1956,
Money, Interest and Prices, Oxford.

(29) Radner, R., 1968,
'Competitive equilibrium under uncertainty', *Econometrica*, 36, 31-58.

(30) Radner, R., 1974,
'Market equilibrium and uncertainty: concept and prob-
lems', in: *Frontiers of Quantitative Economics*, Vol. II,
M.D. Intriligator and D.A. Kendrick (eds.), 43-90.

(31) Robbins, L.R., 1969,
An essay on the nature and significance of economic science,
London.

(32) Rothbard, M.N., 1963,
America's Great Depression, Kansas City.

(33) Sandler, T., 1978,
'Public goods and theory of second best', *Public Finance*,
33, 331-334.

(34) Scherer, F.M., 1979,
Industrial market structure and economic performance,
Chicago.

(35) Shephard, W.G., 1979,
   The Economics of Industrial Organization, Englewood Cliffs.
(36) Starret, P., 1979,
   'Second best welfare economics in the mixed economy', *Journal of Public Economics*, 12, 329-349.
(37) Stigler, G.J., 1968,
   The organization of industry, Homewood.
(38) Walras, L., 1954,
   Elements of pure economics, translated by W. Jaffe, Norwich.
(39) Walsh, J.P., 1982,
   'On deriving pricing rules in the theory of the second best', *Public Finance Quarterly*, 10, 449-509.
(40) Weintraub, E.R., 1979,
   Microfoundations, Cambridge.
(41) Weiszäcker, C.C. von, 1980,
   Barriers to entry, a theoretical treatment, Berlin.

On the authors

Wil Albeda (1925) is president of the Scientific Council for Government Policy (WRR) of the Netherlands and Professor of Social Economic Policy at the University of Limburg (NL). He studied economics in Rotterdam and after a career in the trade union movement became professor at Erasmus University Rotterdam in 1966. Between 1977 and 1981 he was Minister of Social Afffairs.

J.A.H. Maks is associate professor at the Department of Economics of the University of Groningen (NL) and his research interests include applied consumption and production analysis, industrial economics and neo-Austrian economics. His publications include: a paper related to the paper in this volume, entitled "First-best'-regels en de markteconomie" in J.A.H. Maks and E. Wester, eds., *Met het oog op de werkelijkheid, Opstellen over economie en beleid van F. Hartog*, 1983; and a publication on consumption analysis, entitled "A non-Parametric Approach to Demand Behaviour in the Netherlands, 1951-1977", forthcoming in the *European Economic Review*.

Joan Muysken (1948) studied quantitative economics at the University of Groningen and was appointed Professor of Economics at the University of Limburg (NL) in 1984. His dissertation and several other papers are concerned with the aggregation of production functions. Other research work is concentrated on unemployment. Recent publications include: H. v.d. Burg, S.K. Kuipers, J. Muysken and C. de Neubourg, *The Volume and Composition of Structural Unemployment in the Netherlands, 1950-1980*, Den Haag (NPAO), 1982 and H-J. Wagener, J. Muysken, Zur Verlangsamung der dynamischen Effizienz in kapitalistischen und sozialistischen Ländern, in A. Schüller (ed.), Wachstumsverlangsamung und Konjunkturzyklen in unterschiedlichen Wirtschaftssystemen, Berlin, 1984.

Chris de Neubourg (1951) studied economics and sociology at the Universities of Louvain and Antwerp (B). He lectured at the University of Groningen (NL) and is now teaching economics at the University of Limburg (NL). His research efforts are concentrated on labour market issues, including unemployment and labour utilisation, studied in an international comparative context. Recent publications include: *Labour Market Accounting and Labour Utilisation*, Government Publishing Office, The Hague 1983; Aggregate Unemployment and Labour Slack as Indices of Labour Utilisation, in:

D. Bosworth, D.F. Heathfield, *Measuring Capacity and Factor Utilisation*, MacMillan, London 1985; with L. Kok, *Projecting Labour Supply: methods, theory and research: an international comparison*, Government Publishing Office, The Hague (O.S.A.) 1985.

David Plotke is Assistant Professor of Political Science at Yale University. He is completing a study of the Democratic Party, *The Democratic Political Order, 1932-1972*. He is also working on a study of political power in an American post-industrial community. He was editor of *Socialist Review*, co-edited a collection on socialist and communist parties in Western Europe, and has published articles and reviews on American political parties and ideologies, and on contemporary political and social theory.

Joop Roebroek (1951) studied economics and political science at the Catholic University of Nijmegen (NL) where he lectured from 1978 to 1983. Since 1983 he has participated in the research project entitled 'The Development of Social Security Systems in some Western European Countries: a Comparative Study', financed by the Dutch Council for Social Studies (ZWO) and worked on a study for the Ministry of Social Affairs and Employment on 'The Future of Social Security: Social Relations of Force and Political Demands'. In 1983 he published with drs D. Jacobs *Nieuwe sociale bewegingen in Vlaanderen en Nederland*. Since 1985 he works as associate professor at the Department of Social Security Science of the University of Tilburg.

Göran Therborn (1941) is a Swedish sociologist who has been Professor of Political Science at the Catholic University of Nijmegen (NL) since 1982. Besides in Sweden, he has worked in Australia, Canada, France, Mexico and the United States. His publications include: *Science, Class and Society*, (1976), *What Does The Ruling Class Do When It Rules* (1978), *The Ideology of Power and the Power of Ideology* (1980), *Le defi socio-democrate* (1981) and *Why Are Some Peoples More Unemployed Than Others* (1985).

Hans-Jürgen Wagener (1941) studied economics and sociology in Munich and Berlin, and has worked at the Osteuropa Institut of Munich and at the Vienna Institute for International Economic Comparisons. In 1975 he was appointed Professor of Economics at the University of Groningen (NL). His main field of interest is comparative economics. He has published numerous articles and several books, including: "Wirtschaftswachstum in unterentwickelten Gebieten" (Berlin 1972), "Zur Analyse von Wirtschaftssystemen" (Berlin 1979), "The Economic Law of Motion of Modern Society" (Cambridge 1985, with J.W. Drukker).